CONTEMPORARY ARCHITECTURE IN TURIN

EDITED BY GIOVANNI DURBIANO

D1798239

The series "Contemporary Architecture in Turin"
has been realised thanks to support from
the Urban Center Metropolitano of Turin.

www.urbancenter.to.it

MICHELE BONINO

THE PALAZZO DEI LAVORI PUBBLICI: CLIENTS, DESIGNERS, DECISION MAKERS

UMBERTO ALLEMANDI & C.

TURIN ~ LONDON ~ VENICE ~ NEW YORK

English translation
Harriet Graham

On the cover
The facade of the Palazzo dei Lavori Pubblici from the Cathedral.

Contents

I. Seventy years of architecture for Piazza San Giovanni and the archaeological area: the place and its importance (1935-2006)

During the twentieth century, the area in front of the late fifteenth-century Cathedral of Turin, dedicated to St John the Baptist, and the adjacent Roman archaeological area were the object of important changes. Throughout the preceding centuries, the area had maintained a recognizable possibility for a future identity, despite its extremely intricate urban make-up (compared to the geometrical grid of the old centre, it was most irregular)[1] and social diversity, which combined leader roles with a long-established popular following. With the new Cathedral, and later bishops' palaces and buildings annexed to the Royal Palace, built on the site of the three early Christian basilicas of San Salvatore, San Giovanni and Santa Maria, the area consolidated its role of main religious centre in Turin over the centuries.[2]

The Savoy dynasty had clear town planning ideas: the area of San Giovanni became an integral part of the city's power nucleus, its "command zone", its centre of government and seat of the court.

Over the centuries, this resolve led to ambitious proposals, put forward by Carlo di Castellamonte (for the "house of columns" built in about 1622, and for the extension project to the north of the Carignano palaces), by Luigi Canina and by Alessandro Antonelli. Among these:

> Some projects reveal the hypothesis that Piazza Castello, created in the seventeenth century not only as the heart of the command zone but also as a "linking space" between a group of different urban parts under construction, could be connected to other spaces and other public buildings to form an autonomous and even more intricate "central system". The area of the Cathedral has usually been seen as essential to this design.[3]

The 1930s saw a flurry of decisions about this area that were to alter its

TORINO · ZONA DI COMANDO ·
fine del secolo XVIII

1   Palazzo   Reale
2   Palazzo   Vecchio
3   Duomo di S. Giovanni
4   Palazzo del Duca di Genova
5   Chiesa di S. Lorenzo
6   Palazzo Madama
7   Segreterie di Stato
8   Teatro Regio
9   Archivio di Stato
10 Accademia Militare
11 Cavallerizza Reale
12 Cavallerizza Chiablese
13 Zecca e Stamperia Reale
14 Università
15 Seminario arcivescovile

Mario Passanti, the "command zone" of the city of Turin at the end of the eighteenth century; drawing published in M. Passanti, *Architettura in Piemonte*, Turin 1945.

gradual centuries-old urban progress. In 1935, in favour of expropriation and demolition, the Municipality suggested to the Province of Turin that its new offices could be built in place of the high-density block of Santa Lucia, right in front of the Cathedral. In December, as the provincial Technical Office was drawing up a preliminary project, demolition commenced, including Castellamonte's "house of columns" that faced the square with its arcades.

A few months earlier, an ambitious competition brief had been proclaimed and twenty projects submitted, assessed by a jury dominated by the figure of Gustavo Giovannoni representing the High Council of Antiquities and Fine Arts. But no project won:

> The specific difficulty the competition architects had to contend with was [...] the great height of the main facade of the building: this resulted in [...] a cumbersome volume out of proportion with the square and with its principal monument, the delicate and mild Cathedral.[4]

Which approach would prevail in the competition brief, and in the architects' answers? In 1934, in the magazine *Casabella*, Giuseppe Pagano praised the architecture of the Porte Palatine (or Roman Gates to the city), newly restored (for the occasion of the bimillenary of Augustus), as "functional *par ecellence*, monumental for political reasons, and beautiful in their building honesty".[5] But the competition brief of the following year did not include them as central elements to the competition and nor did the architects' proposals reveal any interest in the archaeological area bordering on the site in question. Armando Melis's comment, in his analysis of the results in the pages of *L'Architettura Italiana*, is revealing:

> The square of the Cathedral of Turin is a complex that merits careful attention [...] The fifteenth-century Cathedral, in marble, with a free-standing brick bell tower, completed by a Baroque belfry, stands on the east side. To the south is Palazzo Chiablese [...] and, beyond the start of Via XX Settembre, the side facade of the Palazzo del Seminario Arcivescovile to a beautiful design by Juvarra. On the west, a modest arcaded house now in course of demolition [Castellamonte's "house of columns"] [...], between

Excavations to uncover the archaeological zone on the site of the future Piazza Cesare Augusto, on the occasion of the bimillenary of Augustus.

two streets, the Via Quattro Marzo beautifully sited in line with the Chapel of the Holy Shroud in the Cathedral and the Via della Basilica in line with the bell tower.[6]

As Melis anticipated in his description, the projects of 1935 prioritised the more representative places of the city's command zone, through emphasis on views of Guarini's dome from Via IV Marzo and of the bell tower from Via della Basilica, and the inclusion of the new wing of the Royal Palace. Marginally positioned compared to these monuments, the building for the Provincia was receptive to few other possible urban stimuli.

The project by Mario Passanti, future designer of the Palazzo dei Lavori Pubblici (or municipal office building for Public Works) that would be built on this lot more than twenty years later, did not diverge from this logic. His project did not try to define new urban relationships through views and alignments, but to pursue them physically, "bring-

Views of the square before the demolition of 1935 to make room for the Palazzo della Provincia.

The Santa Lucia block and Carlo di Castellamonte's "house of columns" (*c.* 1622), which stood on the lot of the present Palazzo dei Lavori Pubblici of the City of Turin. The photographs on these two pages were enclosed with the competition brief for the Palazzo della Provincia in 1935.

ing" the space of the Cathedral nave into the new building: two atriums and a court were in fact arranged along its axis, recalling the width of the Cathedral. Faithful to this choice, his project was the only one (together with one by Arturo Midana and Paolo Perona) that positioned the entrance on a line with the entrance to the Cathedral, and not symmetrically on the facade. Passanti was one of the few architects to focus on the street behind: the majority of the projects, with their bulky proposals, helped to worsen the view of the Roman Gate, "located over there lower down".[7]

Perona's project provided an interesting solution to the problem of the height of the building, planning to eliminate the obtuse angle between the square and Via IV Marzo by extending the main facade in an undisturbed curve. Consequently, "the uniformity of the two fronts would give the building a harmonious and tranquil rhythm, to the advantage of the square as well as the building, whose considerable height would be bet-

Mario Passanti, competition project for the Palazzo della Provincia in Turin, entered under the name of "Piemonte reale", 1935.

ter balanced against the surrounding elements in a longer elevation".[8] After a new competition phase, on 12 October Mario Faravelli from Milan was pronounced the winner and was asked for two more detailed projects, then halted by the war.

By this time the area was empty and in 1941 the first negotiations for its conveyance were begun. As discussions continued during the war between the Province and the City, a number of other claimants came forward from the Associazione della Stampa Subalpina to the Opera Diocesana. On 25 August 1950, the Provincial Deputation allowed the Municipality of Turin to use the land as a public rubbish tip.[9]

In 1949, plate 211 of the Reconstruction Plans of the city focussed on the "linking area between Porta Palazzo and Piazza Castello", heavily bombed during the war. But, even in the terms chosen to describe this urban issue ("linking area"), the Reconstruction Plan ignored the stratification of meanings and the importance of this urban fabric, using the war damage as an excuse for accelerating the hypotheses (already partly proposed in the 1930s) for cutting new roads through the historic centre. The plate placed the future Palazzo dei Lavori Pubblici in a central position:[10] but apart from this 'drawn' centrality the Plan in fact obliged the lot in front of the Cathedral to play a marginal role. Before the war it was considered dependent on the Royal Palace complex, existing behind it,[11] whereas now it played a completely different sort of secondary role: in this

Arturo Midana and Paolo Perona, competition project for the Palazzo
della Provincia in Turin, entered under the name of "San Giovanni", 1935.

case, subordinate to the archaeological zone that was gradually attract-
ing increasing attention from city administrators and inhabitants.

The first and important consequence of this residual position, in both
symbolic and physical terms, was a reduction in the surface area of the
lot: it was cut and reduced by axes according to reasoning that had nothing to do with the morphology of the lot but was connected to factors such
as the 'new' monumental importance of the Porte Palatine or the traffic
system. Suffice to think that the block of Santa Lucia demolished in 1935
measured 4047 square metres; 1059 of these were ceded to the Municipality for road widening, provided for by the plan in act; of the remain-
ing 3000, only 2296 were actually to be built on according to the
Province's competition brief. After road alterations established by the Reconstruction Plan, in 1956, the project by Passanti, Perona and Garbaccio had 2234.60 to work with, of which barely 1321.60 were in fact
covered.[12]

In the complex procedures that led to definitive approval of the Reconstruction Plan for the central district in 1954,[13] the area of the future
building was rarely mentioned, almost forgotten, and quite empty since
1935 (being used as a rubbish tip). Its role and nature were not considered crucial for the relevant town planning decisions being formulated.

In 1955, after a protracted exchange, the area passed to the City for the
new building of the Technical and Administrative Offices of Public

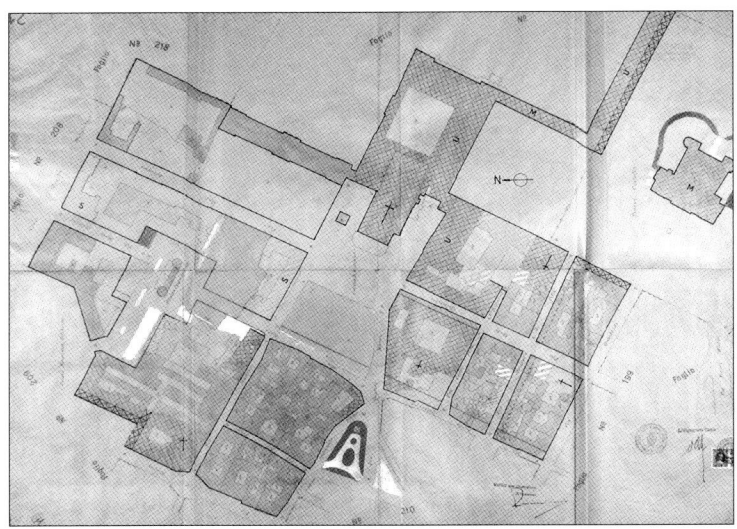

Survey of war damage carried out by the City of Turin in the
"linking area between Porta Palazzo and Piazza Castello", 1949.

Piazza San Giovanni empty; it remained like this from 1935 to the beginning
of construction work on the Palazzo dei Lavori Pubblici in 1960.

Works, since it was deemed "the most suitable for such a purpose, due to its central position and nearness to Palazzo di Città [city government]". With the 1956 competition the ten-year process of constructing the building began.[14] Its construction raised new, almost antithetical, issues compared to those that had been debated following the competition for the Provincia building: the rhetoric and authority of the Fascist Regime were now completely transformed. For the simplicity of the materials used and the building solutions adopted, the chosen solution indicated a government that was much more accessible and closer to its citizens' needs. This objective became the reason for the long-term conflict in which opposing opinions wanted instead to privilege the rhetorical-representative aspects with a 'monumental' front to the building, which would be continually revised up to a total of twelve variations. This was not the only building to suffer such a fate: regarding a project for new houses presented by the architects Ferrero and Foà to redefine the street front of Via Egidi, the Monuments Office stated that it was "absolutely necessary for the issue to be studied not from the stance of an anonymous

The Cathedral of San Giovanni on the eve of the war, with the large square in front of it.

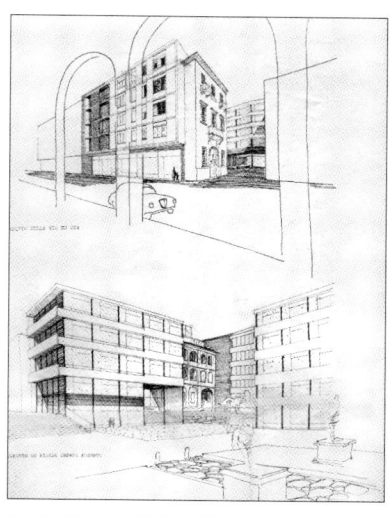

Studio Ferrero-Foà, residential projects for the Porte Palatine area, next to the "casa del Tasso", c. 1952.

View of the Cathedral from the arcade of the Palazzo dei Lavori Pubblici of the City of Turin, by Mario Passanti, Paolo Perona and Giovanni Garbaccio, 1956-1966.

suburban building programme, but as one of the most important and topical problems of the city's town planning, capable of providing the first valid and definitive starting point for ane architectural solution to the new district".[15] Slightly to the north, the building designed by Franco Bassano and Ettore Cometto, the future notary archives, crossed and incorporated the Roman walls. Despite the negative reaction of Superintendences and Ministries, the building was completed in the early 1960s.

The symbolic expectations for the site became stronger: important restoration work on the historic buildings of the area, damaged during the war, was started at the same time as the project for the Public Works building. Between February 1958 and the autumn of 1959 the Palazzo del Seminario Arcivescovile was restored. In 1959 work ended on the Royal Palace and Palazzo Chiablese was restored between 1955 and 1958.

In 1959, the new City Town Plan incorporated the directions of the Reconstruction Plan and, in the following years, new proposals were put forward for an urban area that would remain unresolved and not completed for many years. Studies for the Detailed Plan by Roberto Gabet-

The Palazzo dei Lavori Pubblici soon after it was inaugurated; view from
Via IV Marzo towards the Cathedral with Guarini's dome, 1966.

The same view as the one above
before the demolition of
the Santa Lucia block, 1935.

ti, Giancarlo De Carlo and Giuseppe
Varaldo date to 1967, proposing a direct connection with the gardens of the
Royal Palace. In 1971, the Municipal
Technical Office (councillor Giovanni Astengo) drew up a new Plan
for the area.

The idea for creating an Antiquities
Museum adjacent to the Public
Works building, as in the Plan, was
instead transformed into the construction of an underground building by
Gabetti and Isola along the axis of the
new wing of the Royal Palace, in
1983. The Public Works building became the symbol of many disregarded
predictions: just as the north facade
was planned to relate to an adjacent

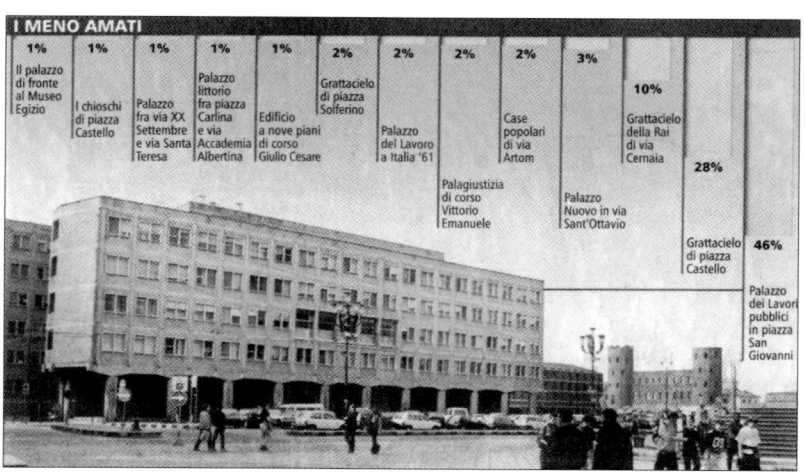

Roberto Gabetti and Aimaro Isola, extension of the Antiquities Museum, 1983.

I MENO AMATI

1%	1%	1%	1%	1%	2%	2%	2%	2%	3%	10%	28%	46%
Il palazzo di fronte al Museo Egizio	I chioschi di piazza Castello	Palazzo fra via XX Settembre e via Santa Teresa	Palazzo littorio fra piazza Carlina e via Accademia Albertina	Edificio a nove piani di corso Giulio Cesare	Grattacielo di piazza Solferino	Palazzo del Lavoro a Italia '61	Case popolari di via Artom			Grattacielo della Rai di via Cernaia		
							Palagiustizia di corso Vittorio Emanuele	Palazzo Nuovo in via Sant'Ottavio			Grattacielo di piazza Castello	Palazzo dei Lavori pubblici in piazza San Giovanni

Survey in *La Stampa*, "The 'least loved' buildings in the city", May 2001. Forty-six per cent of those interviewed voted for the Palazzo dei Lavori Pubblici.

Antiquities Museum, the west front was designed to look onto a never realised road passing through the historic centre, onto which the atrium axis was meaninglessly lined up.

Over the years, the building became a focus for heated debate that involved intellectuals, administrators and above all the populace. The most diverse proposals were advanced for resolving its difficult relationship with the facade of the Cathedral. Mario Fazio, in *Processo all'architettura contemporanea*,[16] pointed to the building as one of the most controversial cases on a national level, and called for its demolition. But architects (note the stance taken by the professional Association) continued to support it, while Turin's inhabitants dreamt up the most extraordinary manifestations: for example, an optician's produced an image of a park in place of the building, calling for a public appeal to the mayor ⸗ "Let's look at Turin through different eyes: down with the Palazzaccio [as the building was commonly called]". The debate, unfortunately often simplified to mere aesthetic considerations, did nothing more in actual fact than emphasise the provisional nature of the city's town planning arrangement. For years the object of architecture degree theses and university lectures, the problem was tackled in a study on residential opportunities in the Roman 'square city', commissioned in 1999 by the Compagnia di San Paolo from a group coordinated by Roberto Gabetti: in this case, it was proposed to surround the building with tall trees.

Later, in 2002, a competition was proclaimed for the archaeological area alone. The ambitious idea was that the complex of buildings and galleries making up the "command zone" might become a single large museum system, from Piazza Castello to the archaeological area, eliminating surface cars with the new underground Santo Stefano car park.

The guide lines, drawn up by the winners Aimaro Isola, Giovanni Durbiano and Luca Reinerio and then developed through coordination with the Technical Offices,[17] departed from the difference in level of about four metres between Piazza San Giovanni and Corso Regina Margherita, with the average height located on a level with the Roman layer. The project lowered the part on top of the old Roman city, included between Via Porta Palatina, the Roman wall, Via XX Settembre and Via della Basilica, to this level, while raising the area outside the Roman

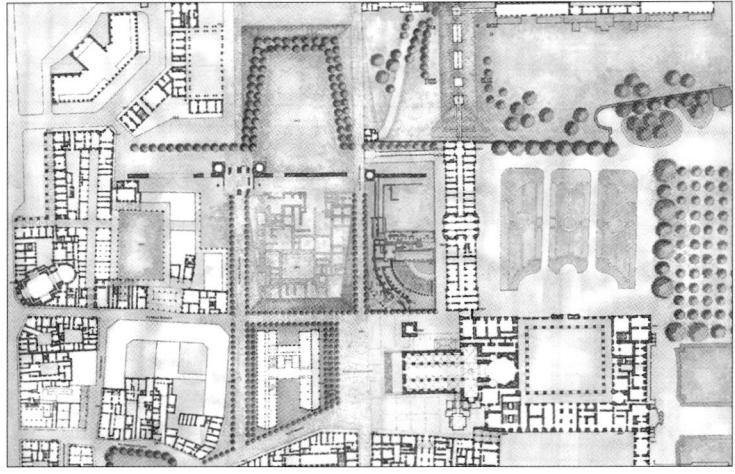

Giovanni Durbiano, Roberto Gabetti, Luigi Falco, Aimaro Isola, Luca Reinerio and Riccarda Rigamonti, "Study for residential opportunities in the Roman area of Turin's historic centre", commissioned by the Compagnia di San Paolo, 1999.

walls: this created a single horizontal plane of green garden that extended towards Corso Regina Margherita to form a bastion, on the line of the
city walls demolished in the nineteenth century. Below this, the market
carts from the neighbouring Porta Palazzo city market were given shel-
ter. The Public Works building was integrated in this overall design,
surrounded by the same colonnade that delimited the garden of the archaeological area. The 'H' plan was bound to that of a closed block by
the uninterrupted pitches of the roof, first in stone slabs and then in glass.[18]
After heated discussion and the presentation of various opinions in view
of the 2006 Winter Olympic deadline, the Municipality chose merely to
subject the building to conservative restoration. The upper crowning element was restored to its original form, and the brickwork was cleaned.
The undressed concrete, a distinctive mark of a non-rhetorical building,
was reintegrated but then covered with plaster.

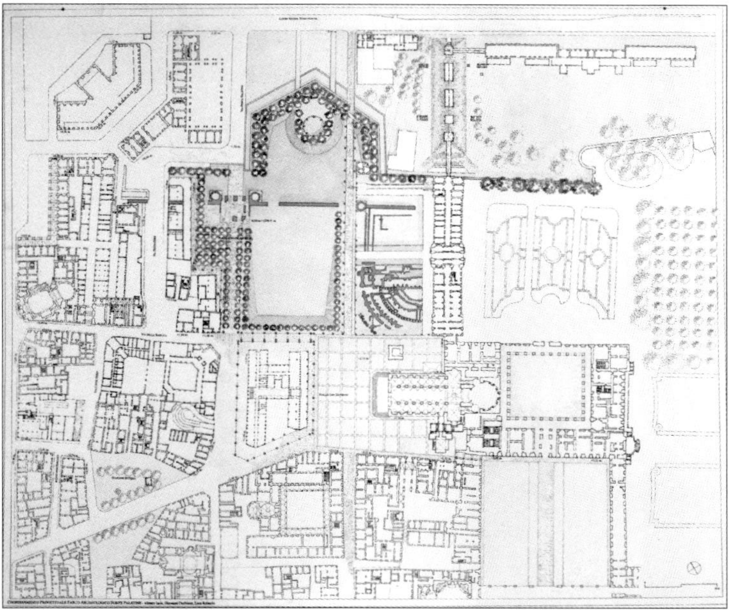

Aimaro Isola, Giovanni Durbiano and Luca Reinerio,
"Layout for the archaeological area", first version, 2003.

View of Piazza San Giovanni from the north: from the left, the Cathedral
of San Giovanni, Palazzo Chiablese, the Seminario Arcivescovile, the Palazzo
dei Lavori Pubblici, the new hotel designed by Gabetti & Isola with Franco Fusari,
and the "casa del Pingone". In the foreground, the Roman wall.

[1] See D. Vitale, *Forma e piano della città. La zona archeologica di Torino*, lecture notes for the course of Architectural Planning I, academic year 1988/1989, Faculty of Architecture, Polytechnic of Turin, p. XVIII. "Due to greater transience in the urban fabric, and also to the lie of the land and the fact that it was on the borders of the city, the topography of this area changed more here than in other areas, moving away from the Roman grid".

[2] Ibid.

[3] Ibid., p. XIX.

[4] Archivio Storico della Provincia di Torino [ASPT], cat. 11/01, 6671, fasc. 126, *Relazione 20 novembre 1935*, p. 6.

[5] G. Pagano, "La Porta Palatina a Torino. Architettura polemica dell'epoca romana", in *Casabella*, 76, April 1934, pp. 34/35.

[6] A. Melis, "Concorso per il progetto per il Palazzo per gli Uffici della Provincia a Torino", in *L'Architettura Italiana*, January 1936, pp. 11/23.

[7] Archivio Mario Passanti [AMP], cart. A45, undated typewritten report.

[8] ASPT, cat. 11/01, 6671, fasc. 126, *Relazione* cit.

[9] ASPT, cat. 11/01, fasc. 129, abstract of the minutes no. 21, session of 25 August 1950.

[10] Archivio Storico della Città di Torino [ASCT], Verbali Consiglio Comunale [VCC], 1949, $13, all. 24, verb. XLVI.

[11] See M. Passanti, *Architettura in Piemonte: da Emanuele Filiberto all'Unità d'Italia (1563/1870)*, Libreria Tecnica Editrice, Turin 1945; republished, edited by G. Torretta, Allemandi, Turin 1990.

[12] Information drawn from a comparison between the two competition briefs and from subsequent project reports.

[13] For further information, see chapter II in this volume. See also M. Bonino, *Mario Passanti Architetto: un'idea di mestiere, 1949/1964*, doctoral thesis in the History of Architecture and Town Planning, Polytechnic of Turin, 2004, in particular chapter II.

[14] For further information, see chapter IV in this volume. For the design and construction work see also Bonino, *Mario Passanti Architetto* cit., chap. I; see also A. De Rossi, M. Robiglio and M. Siracusa, "Due progetti per la Piazza San Giovanni a Torino", in R. Rigamonti (ed.), *Mario Passanti, architetto docente universitario*, Celid, Turin 1995.

[15] Letter from the head of Monuments Umberto Chierici of 13 September 1955, to the mayor of Turin and the Ministry of Education.

[16] See M. Fazio, *Passato e futuro delle città. Processo all'architettura contemporanea*, Einaudi, Turin 2000; chap. IV: "Dinamite per i 'mostri'?", p. 92, fig. 11.

[17] Egidio Cupolillo was responsible for the project; the designer was Paola Giordano.

[18] See A. Isola, G. Durbiano and L. Reinerio, "Il nuovo Parco archeologico della Porta Palatina", in L. Mercando (ed.), *Archeologia a Torino*, Allemandi, Turin 2003, pp. 333/345.

II. The urban prerequisites of the Palazzo dei Lavori Pubblici: the difficult evolution of the Reconstruction Plan (1949-1954)

During the years following Liberation, and with no new Town Plan capable of accommodating the radical transformations in the city induced by war damage (a new Plan would be approved only in 1959, replacing the one of 1906), Reconstruction Plans became the most effective instruments for town planning management: to the degree that even new areas of urbanisation would be subject to these mechanisms, such as the districts of Falchera and Mirafiori Sud.

Although a national law[1] in 1945 included Turin among the municipal districts that had to adopt such Plans, the Municipal Council managed to approve them for only five districts of the city on 22 October 1949. Among these areas, the central district included the issue of the "linking area between Porta Palazzo and Piazza Castello": but, after heavy bombing during the war, its problems seemed so complex that the minister for Public Works, Salvatore Aldisio, in approving the Plans with a decree of 10 February 1951, removed just the master plate 211 and the relative building norms, maintaining that it was impossible "to disregard the environmental factors that the plan neglects, while anticipating the extension of roads and spaces, defined too rigidly by new buildings completely foreign to the environment in which they should be inserted".[2]

This was the first act in a dialogue that would indelibly mark the development of these areas, and which would see the municipal authorities facing the High Council of Public Works, the advisory body of the Ministry of the same name. The relationship with Rome was always decisive, and the resulting indications would be interpreted differently every time: sometimes placed on the table of the Municipal Council as a legitimising element; at others, taken as a cause for delay and a disturbance to com-

monly agreed local positions; at yet others, due to the authority or pres-
tige of some council members, capable of questioning objectives that were
already considered firmly established by Turin's decision makers. Some
figures of intellectual importance took on leading roles within the Council, who over the years produced a recognisable though not united institutional culture. Actors involved in a conflict that was not solely administrative included the minister himself, Aldisio, promoter in 1952 of
the regional plan, Giuseppe Samonà, later Pier Luigi Nervi, and
Guglielmo De Angelis d'Ossat, director of the council of Antiquities
and Fine Arts, who had influential roles in the High Council of Public
Works too.

To stimulate debate after the Plan was rejected, the Provincial Body
for Tourism proclaimed a regional competition in August 1951 for a
project for the buildings surrounding the Porte Palatine and Piazza Cesare Augusto.[3] In November, from analysis of the nine projects presented, the jury drew up some priorities in order to resolve the problems in
the district. Chaired by Giovanni Chevalley,[4] it proposed in order of im-

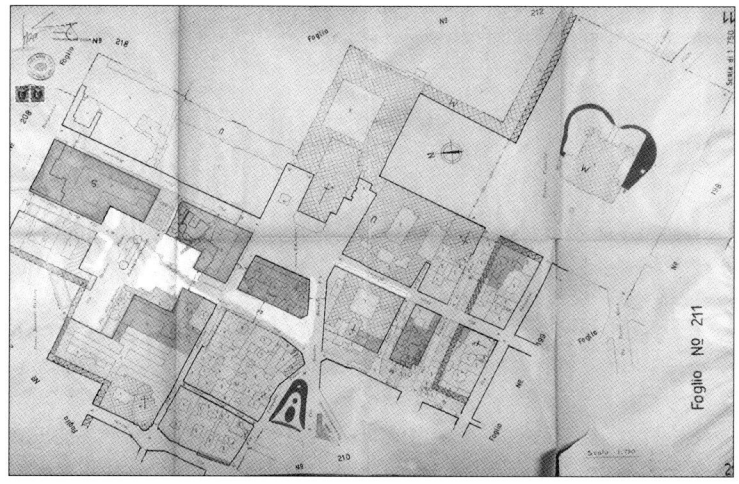

The Reconstruction Plan of the Municipality of Turin: sheet 211, extracted by
the Ministry in 1949. The twenty-four-metre-wide road that was to connect the Porte
Palatine with Piazza Castello through blocks of historic urban fabric is clearly visible.

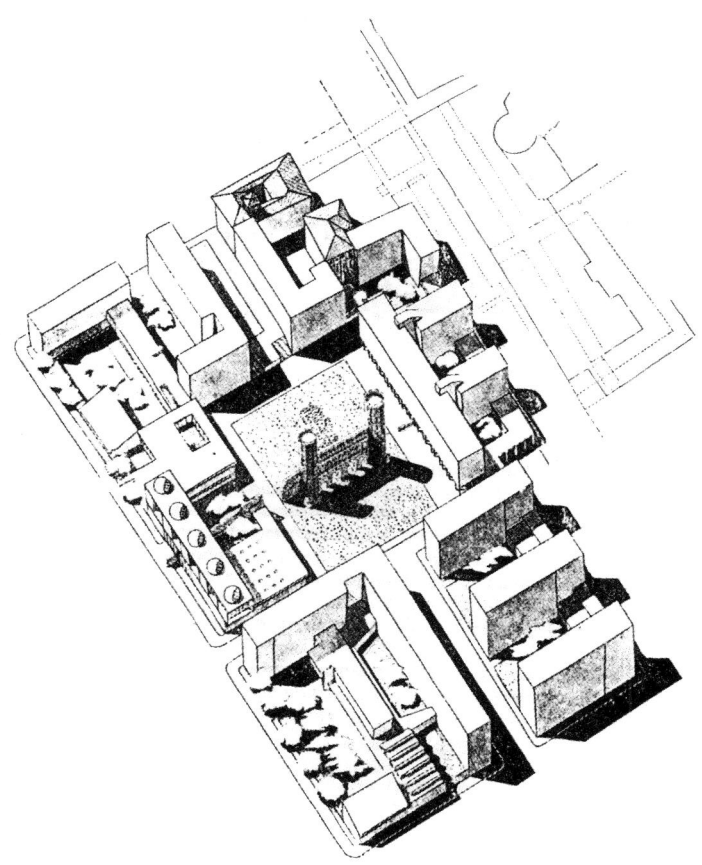

Competition for Piazza Cesare Augusto, 1951. First prize, group of Sergio Nicola, Franco Berlanda and Alberto Todros.

portance to enhance the spatial arrangement of Porta Palatina (the competition brief set the height of the buildings around the square at the level of the walls between the towers); the view of the towers from the nearby roads, to be designated to "tourist traffic"; and a careful arrangement of the building groups around the area of monuments.

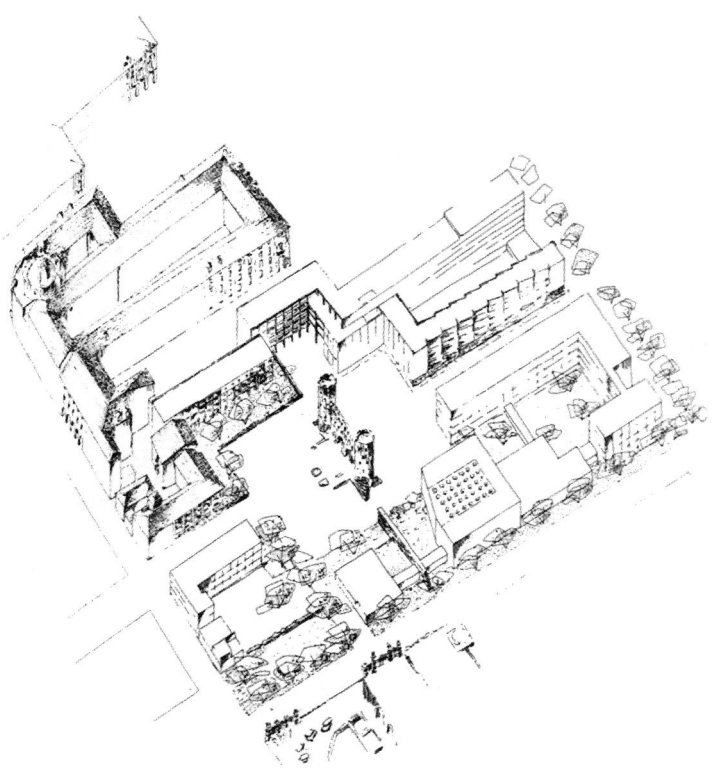

Competition for Piazza Cesare Augusto, 1951.
Fourth prize, group of Roberto Gabetti, Giorgio Raineri and Aimaro Isola.

First prize was awarded to Sergio Nicola, Franco Berlanda and Alberto Todros; second to Augusto Romano. The two projects proposed virtually opposing schemes, which also seemed to underlie the other competition projects. In the first, a square area, concluded to the south by a museum and to the north by new schools, surrounds the towers and does not permit any view of them from the parvis of the Cathedral. However, the jury appreciated the attention paid to the Roman area, with volumes overlooking it that were "prudent and calm" (as the commission explained). Romano, instead, opened up a diagonal that granted a view of the archaeological zone from both the Cathedral steps and from Piazza della Repubblica opposite.

Competition for the cultural zone, 1952. First prize, Annibale Rigotti.

Third were Annibale and Giorgio Rigotti, proposing a solution in line with the winner; fourth were Roberto Gabetti, Giorgio Raineri and Aimaro Isola, who, instead, preferred to follow the second idea but with a solid volume closing the diagonal on the other side of the square.[5]

Both the initiative of this competition and a second competition (this time on a national scale) proclaimed at almost the same time by the same Provincial Tourist Body for the "cultural zone" to the east of Piazza Castello invite reflection on the relationship between politics and city projects, in a comparison of the main public operations under way at the beginning of the 1950s.

In June 1951, Amedeo Peyron was elected mayor.[6] The new Christian Democrat Executive Town Council must be attributed merit for a far-sighted programme that would resolve the ten-year-long problem of the Town Plan, approved at the first vote by the Town Council on 7 April 1956. However, a glance at these years of administration (Peyron would be mayor until 1962) reveals an Executive Council with a weaker planning vision than previous ones, prudently concentrated on realistically balancing the accounts. "Apart from budget ideals, the basic idea was to reduce the activity of the municipal administration in order to lower local taxation".[7] Any ideas for projects and transformation were far from being included in the mandate of this prevailing political-administrative attitude.[8]

In February 1952, the competition for the cultural area was won by Annibale Rigotti, from nineteen projects entered. The buildings involved in the plan were the State Archives, the RAI auditorium, the Teatro Regio opera house, the University, the National Library and the Museum of Turin. An assessment of the developments resulting from this competition for some of the buildings led to a first reckoning about the 'feasibility' of public works in this administrative phase. It was decided to start the reconstruction of the Teatro Regio, already in a study phase before the war after the national competition of 1937 that had awarded the projects by Aldo Morbelli and Rinaldo Morozzo della Rocca. After a total of six designed versions and the foundation stone laid twice in thirty years, with Morbelli dying in the meantime in 1963, the Municipal Council finally, on 25 July 1966, decided to approve the project by Carlo Mollino and Marcello Zavelani Rossi. This was then built and the theatre was inaugurated in 1973.[9] The competition briefs for the National Library (1958) and the Humanities Faculty (1959) were proclaimed only many years after the competition for the cultural area.

While talking of public works, mention must also be made of hospitals and schools, the most urgent and difficult in the reconstruction years. The project for the Martini hospital, following a competition held in 1949,[10] was protracted for the whole of the 1950s under the attention of the High Councils for Health and Public Works. Initial contact was made with INAIL (the national insurance institute for accidents at work) to build the Centro Traumatologico Ortopedico (traumatology and orthopaedic hospital) and a suitable area identified (previously hypothesised for the new Polytechnic) but here too it was necessary to wait for the next decade (1965) before it was built.

In general, the practical skills of a city for any effective implementation in front of the most important urban reconstruction work (the area between Porta Palazzo and Piazza Castello) could be considered weak, although all the leading decision makers and 'politicians' who were shortly to be involved with constructing the Public Works office building in Piazza San Giovanni were already present on the scene - from Peyron to Natale Reviglio, from Chevalley (in his role of president of the executive commission of the Town Plan) to Giancarlo Anselmetti. But, in this

initial phase, no future designers were present: they would
come to a process that had not
been touched by architecture.

In a report of 18 July 1952,
Giovanni Chevalley sum-
marised what had been accepted in the Reconstruction Plan of
the competition for the area of
the Porte Palatine, for which the
jury had stated that "none of the
projects entered [...] combined
all the necessary qualities to be
considered suitable to adopt".

Giovanni Chevalley in the 1930s.

Who was responsible for the Plan that was finally approved, drawn
up without any sign of reference to the results of the competition? A bird's
eye view by Gianni Ricci (an architect favoured by the city's upper middle classes and head of the municipal Technical Offices in these years),
given to Reviglio (councillor for Public Works), shows an urban space
far from the symmetrical monumentality of the solution proposed in 1949.
On the other hand, it was equally distant from the project by Nicola,
Berlanda and Todros that had won the competition:[11] the area of the future office of Public Works is occupied by a building imitating Castellamonte's "house of columns", designed as a closed block.

This was the basis of the project finally drawn up by the Technical Office, accepting the suggestions of the High Council of Antiquities and
Fine Arts: spurred on by Ricci's plan an 'L' shape space was defined for
the Porte Palatine area, where to the north a system of arcades closed the
area around the towers, while green areas extended towards the east to include the Roman amphitheatre and other remains. The level of Via XX
Settembre and all the surrounding area was lowered to the original level
of the Roman city; traffic was excluded as the area was gradually awarded a previously unknown urban importance through the construction of
pedestrian steps and concentrating vehicular flow along the new road towards Piazza Castello, a variant on an earlier planned route which left

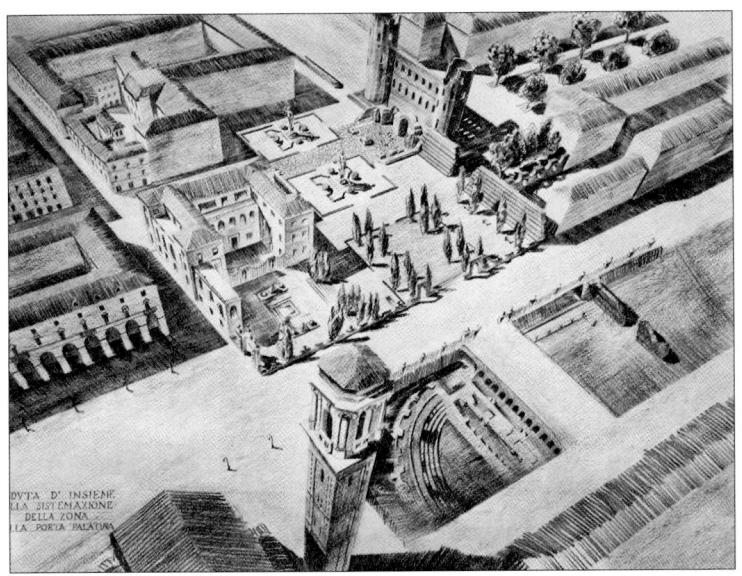

Gianni Ricci, perspective view showing a possible layout for the Porte Palatine area, *c.* 1952. A similar looking courtyard block is proposed in place of Castellamonte's building. On the back: "To my friend Reviglio", councillor for Public Works at that time.

the Roman gates free. Finally a Museum of Antiquities was designated to occupy the block to the north of the future Public Works building, the site of the Torquato Tasso school, seriously damaged and now planned in a position adjacent to Corso Regina Margherita. From the different points emerging from the competition, only the idea of regulating the height of new buildings to the inter-tower wall height of the Porte Palatine was taken up.

The new plan was approved by the Executive Town Council,[12] although it was the object of heated debate in the Town Council before being voted. Indeed, while the planning process dragged on to be finally approved nine years after the end of the war, many houses had already been rebuilt: by the end of 1952, in Via Palazzo di Città alone more than two thousand inhabitants had resettled, and would have to be evicted if the planned measures were applied.[13]

In the Town Council session of 8 October 1952, Reviglio proposed

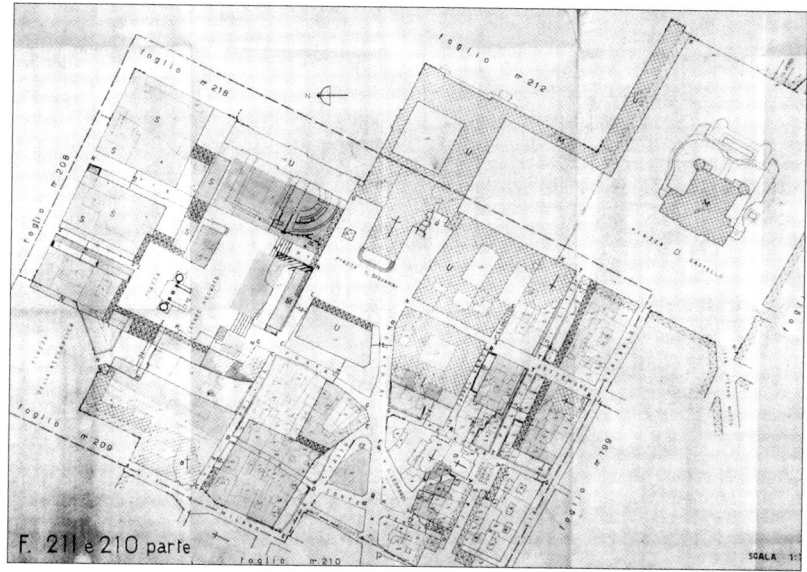

The Reconstruction Plan of the Municipality of Turin: sheet 211, second version, approved by the Town Council in 1952.

approving the resolution, but in the name of the opposition Todros,[14] councillor for the Communist Party and designer of the winning project the previous year, asked the "Councillor to illustrate the phases that had led to the draft of the actual project, since it is completely different from what the competition had asked for". Reviglio emphasised the fact that numerous discussions had led to a mixed solution between the idea of a closed square (awarded in the competition), "which can give the necessary frame to the towers", and one of an open space that "allows a view of the Cathedral and the Royal Palace".[15]

During the thirty days after the Provincial Administrative Council had given its approval (5 November 1952) almost four hundred appeals from property owners in the areas involved were lodged.[16] It was an unpopular Plan, contested by opposing political parties and by townspeople. However, on 23 December 1952 the Municipal Executive Council, thanks to powers obtained in the preceding council resolution, was able to continue with the approval procedures and submit it to the Ministry of Public Works.

Among the counter deductions produced, which especially answered requests for a greater exploitation in height in return for the many demolitions necessary, interesting elements emerge about the area of the future Public Works office building, taken as an example of the inappropriateness of greater building height: the maximum height was fixed at twenty-one metres.

Just one objection, put forward by the Provincial Administration which still owned the area, directly involved this block: criticism was made about widening Via Porte Palatine from ten to twenty-four metres, being obliged to provide arcades fronting the square in reference to Castellamonte's earlier building (a choice that, with the preceding one, considerably reduced the cubic volume of the future building) and the fact that the lot was inserted into a "reconstruction" plan when in fact it had already been demolished before the war. Regarding the arcades, the Executive Council "observes that they already existed in the demolished building and that they are particularly useful for the large numbers of public who will enter or pause before the offices [...] It is also to be hoped that it will be rebuilt as an arcade with coupled columns as in the pre-existing building".

At the beginning of 1954, the Plan was still lying on the Minister's table. The High Council decided to resolve a few points during a site inspection of the area: on 22 February 1954 Giuseppe Samonà, representing the Ministry, met municipal delegates in Turin.[17] After five years of variations, public debate and counter proposals, important decisions were made during the day that would remain impressed on the plates of the Reconstruction Plan. As well as confirming "the need to widen Via Palazzo di Città [...] and Via Porta Palatina up to the line of the apse of the Chapel of the Seminario", the perspective of Via IV Marzo towards the Cathedral was closely examined and as a result the previously planned eighteen-metres' width of this street were reduced.

Approval is given along the old axis for reconstruction of the area facing the Cathedral, limiting the height to just below the eaves of Palazzo del Seminario and preserving Via Basilica on the north side, which can be re-

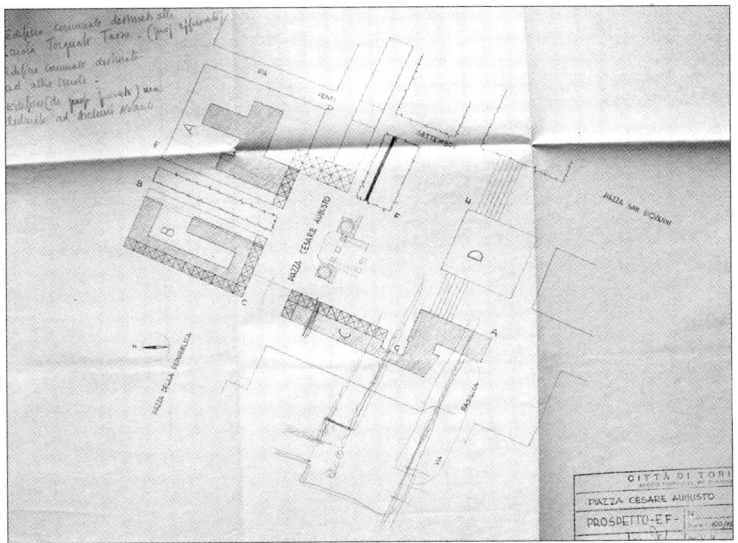

Résumé draft by the Technical Office, after Giuseppe Samonà's visit to the site, undated (1954).

duced in width to a minimum compatible with the height of the street fronts.[18]

Samonà felt it essential to extend the Cathedral square towards the north, incorporating the new wing of the Royal Palace into this public space: the square would thus be closed at the bottom by the school build-ings next to Corso Regina, beyond the towers. In this way, the view from the Cathedral steps to the Porte Palatine was maintained, to the cost of a rather uncertain junction between Piazza San Giovanni and the previ-ously defined 'L' space.

On examining the "casa del Tasso and the "casa del Pingone", con-sidered up till then medieval buildings worth conserving, the Commis-sion believed the latter should be sacrificed: an idea was put forward for a building in its place that would be symmetrical, with respect to the ax-is of Porta Palatina, to the Antiquities Museum (confirmed in writing on returning to the municipal offices).[19]

On 20 July 1954, the Minister of Public Works issued a decree definitively approving the Reconstruction Plan of the area included between Piazza Castello and Porta Palazzo. The clearance hypotheses that had caused the Ministry to reject the plan in 1949 were no longer raised, and would not be in the future either. In 1959 the Reconstruction Plan became law, included in the new General Town Plan.

[1] Decree with the effect of law 1 March 1945, no. 154.

[2] See "I piani di ricostruzione a Torino sono stati approvati dal ministero", in *Gazzetta del Popolo*, 9 August 1951.

[3] Archivio Storico della Città di Torino [Ascт], 717-717/a, *Bando di Concorso per il progetto di Massima Volumetrico ed architettonico della Piazza Cesare Augusto di Torino*, Ente Provinciale per il Turismo, Turin 18 August 1951.

[4] Giovanni Chevalley (1868-1954), professor at the Polytechnic (1912-1932) and at the Accademia Albertina (1926-1927), municipal councillor, several times councillor of Public Works, president of the Società degli Ingegneri e degli Architetti, as well as president of the working committee for Turin's Town Plan and a member of the administrative council of public and private institutions. He was one of the most important decision makers in the city during the first half of the twentieth century. He did in-depth research on Benedetto Alfieri and on the Piedmontese eighteenth century and, as a designer, among other things was responsible for the extension of Palazzo Agnelli in Corso Matteotti (1920-1928), the main branch of the Cassa di Risparmio di Torino (1929-1931), as well as, with Passanti, the Principi di Piemonte hotel in Sestrière (1929).

[5] See A. GUERRA and M. MORRESI (eds.), *Gabetti e Isola: opere di architettura*, Electa, Milan 1996, pp. 15-17.

[6] With the elections of 10 and 11 June 1951 (then reconfirmed in 1956): Peyron was elected to govern the city after seven years of Communist party rule.

[7] M. MORAGLIO, "Amministrazioni locali e infrastrutture a Torino", in F. LEVI and B. MAIDA (eds.), *La città e lo sviluppo. Crescita e disordine a Torino 1945-1970*, Franco Angeli, Milan 2002; pp. 295-329.

[8] See "Il sindaco Peyron annuncia il piano di lavoro per i quattro anni della nuova amministrazione", in *La Stampa*, 21 July 1951.

[9] See R. GABETTI, "Iniziative editoriali per la città: una storia del Teatro Regio", in *Studi Piemontesi*, March 1984.

[10] See M. PASSANTI, "Concorso per il progetto di ricostruzione dell'ospedale Martini in Torino", in *Atti e rassegna tecnica della Società degli Ingegneri e degli Architetti in Torino*, no. 4, V, n.s., April 1951, pp. 109-118.

[11] ASCT, no file number.

[12] Resolution of 25 July 1952.

[13] See "La sistemazione della zona archeologica solleva la protesta di ottomila cittadini", in *La Stampa*, 10 December 1952.

[14] Returning to Italy after being deported to Mauthausen, Alberto Todros (1920-2003) became a member of the federal commission of the Italian Communist Party and in 1951 was elected a municipal councillor in Turin, a position he would hold for 24 years. He was a member of Parliament for four terms from 1963, where he had a position in the Public Works Commission. He was an acting member of the National Institute for Urbanism for many years. As a designer, he drew up the town plans for Alessandria, Vado Ligure, Venaria and Beinasco, took part in drawing up the inter-municipal Plan of Savona and was a member of the study Commission for the inter-municipal Plan of Turin. See also A. TODROS, *Memorie 1920-1952*, Trauben, Turin 1996.

[15] ASCT, Verbali Consiglio Comunale [VCC], 8 October 1952, §4.

[16] Among the appeals, one of the most recurrent criticisms attacked a "reconstruction" plan that in effect completely upset, rather than rebuilt, the urban fabric. It is noteworthy that in the whole city, between 1946 and 1956, 2756 authorisations for added storeys were conceded, 3130 new buildings, but only 367 rebuildings. See A. DE MAGISTRIS, "L'urbanistica della grande trasformazione", in *Storia di Torino*, IX (*Gli anni della Repubblica*), edited by N. TRANFAGLIA, Einaudi, Turin 1999, pp. 189-233.

[17] Others taking part were Carducci and Chierici, the two heads of Roman Antiquities and of Monujments in Piedmont involved, Reviglio, and engineer Giorgio Rigotti as a representative of the Commission for the new Town Plan.

[18] ASCT, no file number, *Verbale del sopraluogo effettuato il 22-2-1954 alla zona della Porta Palatina, dai rappresentanti del Consiglio Superiore dei LL.PP*.

[19] Finally, "architect Samonà proposes, and other members approve, the construction of private houses along the west side to create an uninterrupted front from the 'casa del Tasso' to Corso Regina with arcades and arches aiming at creating a view of the towers from the new parallel artery", ibid.

III. Mario Passanti and an idea of civic architecture (1949-1956)

Mario Passanti (1901-1975) is one of the main figures in this story, winner of the competition for the City Office Building of Public Works in 1956 and then designer of the building together with Paolo Perona, with whom he had worked since the 1930s, and Giovanni Garbaccio. Passanti's career combined an uninterrupted professional practice (over fifty years, from the end of the 1920s to the 1970s) with research, writing, lecturing, and teaching disciplines such as the History of Art and Architecture and Surveying at the Faculty of Architecture in Turin. In 1945, he published *Architettura in Piemonte*, followed by the thirty-year drafting of an extraordinarily rich book, *Genesi e comprensione dell'opera architettonica*, never published except for two short but dense intermediate versions.[1]

Also in the light of these far-ranging interests, Passanti's intellectual position with respect to his profession is worthy of attention. Like others of his generation, "who had an individual creed of commitment, an almost concealed work ethics",[2] he did not impose a theoretician's rigid force nor the charisma of an ideologist in front of practical experience. Instead, he assumed a multi-faceted stance towards the rules of his craft and did not rise against the "common professionalism" pervading reconstruction, preferring to dialogue with norms, bureaucracy and the market. This educated inquiring attitude endowed this dialogue with a realistic quality. In the case of his work on public buildings, this led to his desire to contribute to the representation of a civic authority that approached the citizens more closely. He could interpret this relationship through an idea of 'poverty', and building facility and clarity. At the Falchera, the INA-Casa district completed in the years 1951-1954, Passanti's block was the only one that was immediately contracted out, due

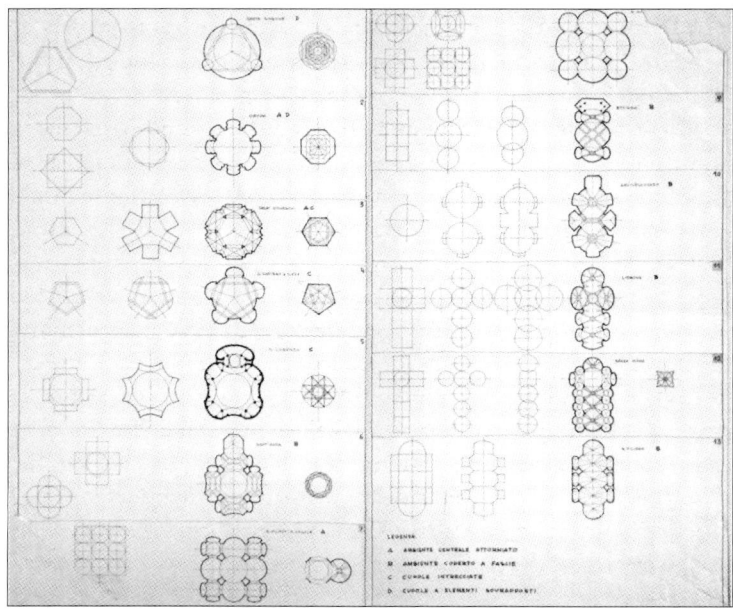

Mario Passanti (with Biagio Garzena), "Types of Guarini churches",
plate published in M. Passanti, *Il Mondo Magico di Guarino Guarini*, Turin 1963.

its plain solutions and clear tender specifications.

These facts are essential to an understanding of the Palazzo dei Lavori Pubblici, within an evolution of thought on public buildings that Passanti devoted himself to intensely from 1949. A solid idea of civic architecture holds together the three versions for the Town Hall of Moncalieri (1949-1950 Passanti and Bonicelli; 1954 Passanti; 1957 Passanti and Luigi Rocca, never built), drafted while Passanti and Perona were designing and building the elementary schools and the theatre not far away; the two versions for the Palazzo della Provincia e della Prefettura di Asti (1955; 1956-1961, with Domenico Schiavinato); and the twelve different variations for the Public Works building in Piazza San Giovanni, Turin (1956-1964, with Perona and Garbaccio).

At Moncalieri, the 1940 bombing of the bridge over the Po (the only direct connection with Turin) led the town administration to commission a new Town Plan from the engineers Andrea Quaglia and Anselmo Moretto, joined later by Carlo Mollino. Drawn up in 1940-1941, it indicated "continuity with the urban centre of Turin" a top priority: a single large municipal square was planned in place of the two former smaller ones on the axis of the new bridge. The Plan set down the alignments and system of arcades on the north side but left the issue of the new fronts undecided. Passanti's project concentrated particularly on this.[3]

At Asti, the site of today's Piazza Alfieri had been the main centre of the town's commercial activities since the middle of the nineteenth century. The 'Alla' (a typical nineteenth-century Piedmontese market building) concluded this triangular space to the south, a position that the Town Plan approved in 1935 destined to be the new Casa Littoria.[4] In 1933, a competition was proclaimed for its design and the architects were given free reign regarding the 'Alla': conservation, demolition or incorporation into the new building. Passanti took part in Giovanni Chevalley's group. Just as he would do for the competition for the Palazzo della Provincia in Piazza San Giovanni, proclaimed the following year, Armando Melis commented the competition results in *L'Architettura Italiana*:[5] the project by Ottorino Aloisio won. Work commenced in 1936, but was halted by the war, leaving the empty space that would be covered by the Palazzo della Provincia e della Prefettura in the 1950s. Passanti was assigned the work, in recognition of his commitment in public and institutional building spheres.

These brief descriptions reveal how both the two 'civic' buildings have a central position in their respective towns, in keeping with their representative role, although both lie on the borders of the true historic centre: for this reason they were particularly exposed to the reconstruction and transformation programmes set in action after the war. Furthermore, all three examples are strongly connected to an important square, with which they seek an explicit dialogue that becomes a central focus of the projects. Other comparisons can also be made when considering the intense search in the early years after the war for a new urban role for public architecture.

A constant in Passanti's research was his desire to contribute to the urban dimension via close and direct continuity with the architectural project. Attracted by those "marvels of the passage between urban element

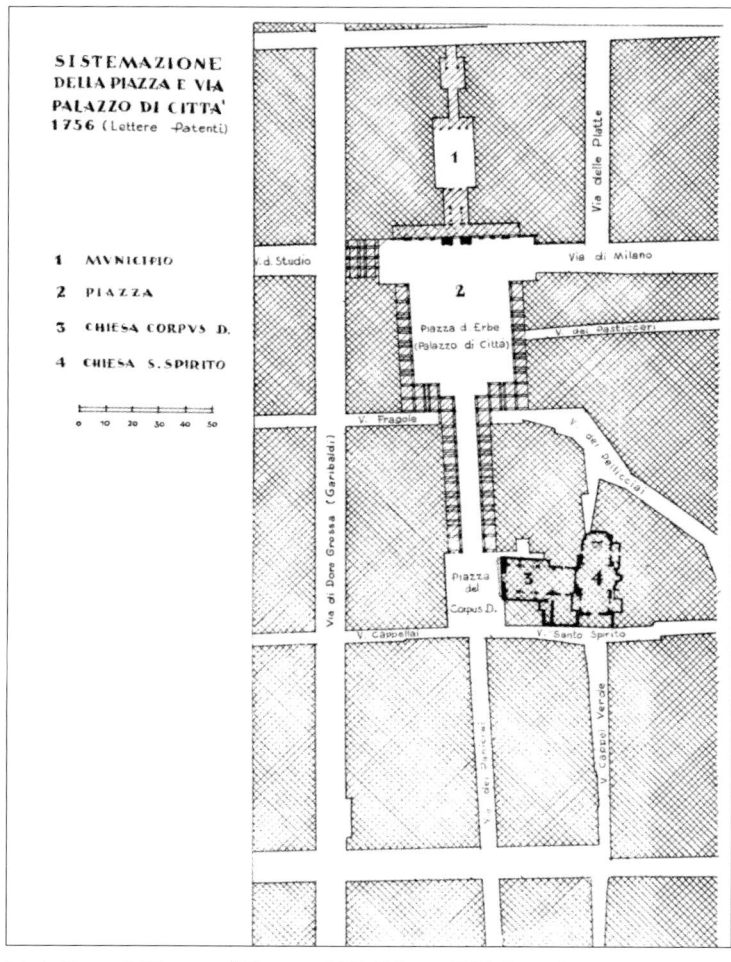

Mario Passanti, "Layout of Piazza and Via Palazzo di Città 1756",
drawing published in M. Passanti, *Architettura in Piemonte*, Turin 1945.

and architectural element",[6] at Moncalieri, Asti and Turin, Passanti
showed that he wanted to interpret stretches of urban fabric as great architecture, and, vice versa, consider individual buildings as functionally
part of the urban fabric, inseparable from it. He explained to his students:

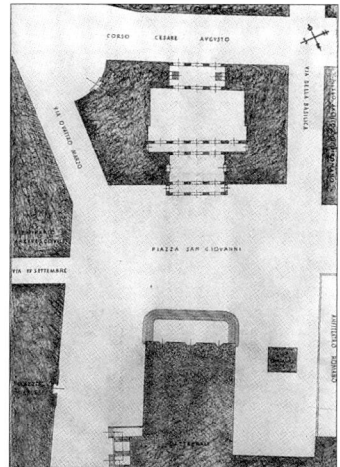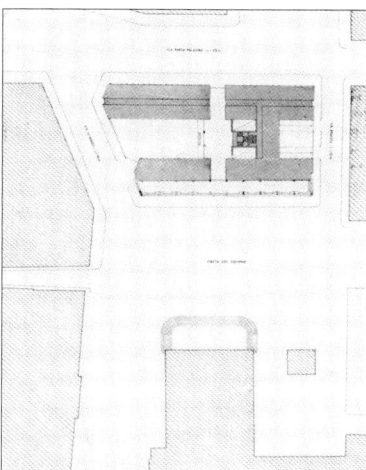

Comparison between the plans by Mario Passanti for the competition for the
Palazzo della Provincia (1935) and for the competition for the
Palazzo dei Lavori Pubblici (with Perona and Garbaccio, 1956).

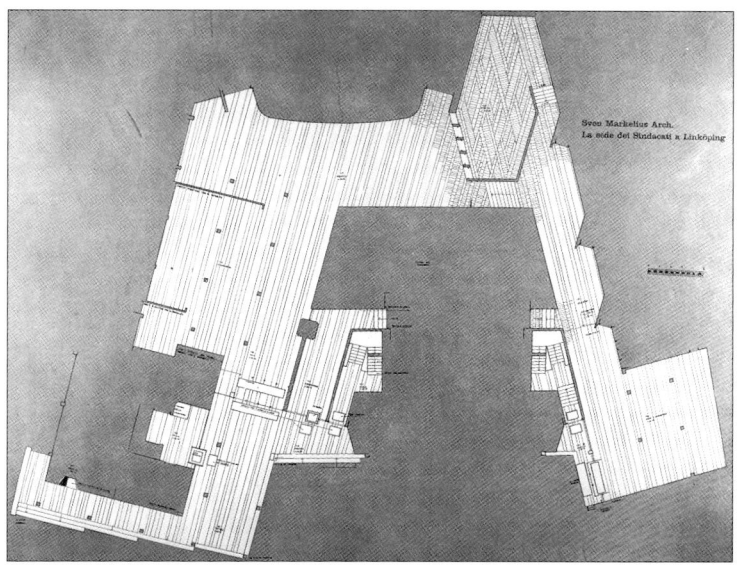

Sven Markelius, 'negative' plan of the union building in Linköping (Sweden),
published in *Casabella - Continuità*, 201, April-May 1954.

We who see new roads emerging [...] in so many different dimensions and in materials that will not change or look the same over time, we now appreciate this road [Via Pietro Micca] for the modesty of the buildings that with smoke, dust, sun and rain now all resemble each other so that the individual decoration has become quite secondary [...] Just as a well educated person immediately converses with every type of person using a tone appropriate to the moment [...], so our buildings, even if they do not manage to be sublime, seek to establish bonds and harmony with all the others [...] In one's early years much importance is given to how we work or we tend to isolate our object when planning [...] As the work progresses one realises that what one does is nothing but a tiny addition to something that persists and only gradually changes.[7]

Daniele Vitale placed Passanti "among the few Italian architects of his generation who have systematically studied the city, making it a reference and basis for their way of working in the meantime".[8] This gave rise to a focus on the urban "site" and to the definition of a field of comparison between one's own practical skills and those deposited in the city and in its buildings: two "analogous skills" that lead to interpreting the city not as a "catalogue" of stylistic or technological solutions but rather as a field for comparison, according to Vitale "a great experience" taken all in all.

This stance becomes more evident if one analyses various drawings that Passanti made to study the city's urban shape: the plan of Piazza Palazzo di Città a Torino highlights this building's public thoroughfare system. This drawing was published in 1945, and is striking for its similarity, both as a drawing and as a building, to the long atrium that would pass through the Public Works building a few years later. A direct contemporary influence for Passanti was the plan of the union building in Linköping (Sweden) by Sven Markelius, published in *Casabella - Continuità* in 1954: in the same way the public space penetrating the building is shown in white, while the private parts are covered in an overall grey.

Analysis of the two projects for Moncalieri and Asti reveals further points of inspiration and reflection, linked not merely to a local dimension. At Moncalieri, the first two versions of the Town Hall (1949-1950 and 1954) refer to very different project ideas (the first, a buildings with a pitch roof and Greek decoration; the second, a juxtaposition of two parallelepiped volumes where the upper body projects on all four sides) but address the same functional layout and in their dialogue with the city reveal similar influences, showing a desire to interpret a still tattered urban fabric after bombing. This was done by means of the double-fronted central atrium, which connects the arcade and road behind, or by making the building an effective part of a pedestrian system that rises towards the upper districts of the town. The third hypothesis (1957) instead was just a scheme, and here Passanti placed greater emphasis on the functions, and on the new relationships to be made with the city and with the square.[9] It hinges on the idea of "centrality" as a new urban function, a build-up of activities and a hub of connections, capable of involving the building in new relationships with the public sphere. This theme was proposed in this period by the 8th CIAM (Congrès Internationaux d'Architecture Moderne), held at Hoddesdon (Great Britain)

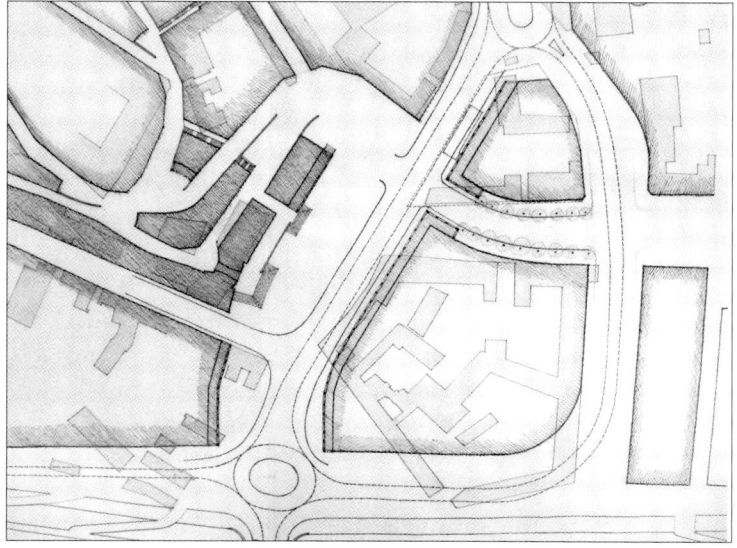

Mario Passanti and G. Bonicelli, project for Moncalieri Town Hall; its position on a plan that includes the directions indicated in the project by Andrea Quaglia, Carlo Mollino and Anselmo Moretto, 1949.

in 1951, developing under the impetus of Josep Lluís Sert and Ernesto Nathan Rogers into a new interest in the *heart of the city*,[10] unknown to the Modern Movement. The notes recorded at the end of the meeting made repeated reference not only to functional objectives but also to a number of symbolic meanings, for a city centre that seemed to have lost its secular significance with modernity.

As pointed out by Ignasi de Solà-Morales,[11] the term "heart", lacking any true definition between functional and symbolic values, characterised this CIAM congress. The speeches "make it clear how the modern city has lost some of its urban values which, with the post-war crisis, are once again felt to be necessary", together with an attempt to understand what it was of traditional cities that really did no longer appear in modern cities.

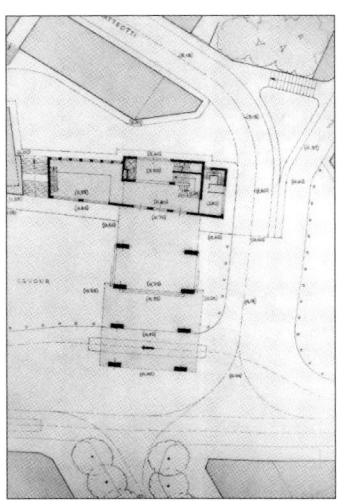

Passanti too did not believe that 'centrality' was a purely functional category, as his dry designs for the Moncalieri Town Hall might show. At Asti, for example, according to the architect:

The arcades devoid of shops, facing north, with the enormous emptiness of the square in front of them, will al-

Mario Passanti and Luigi Rocca, Moncalieri Town Hall, third version, 1957.

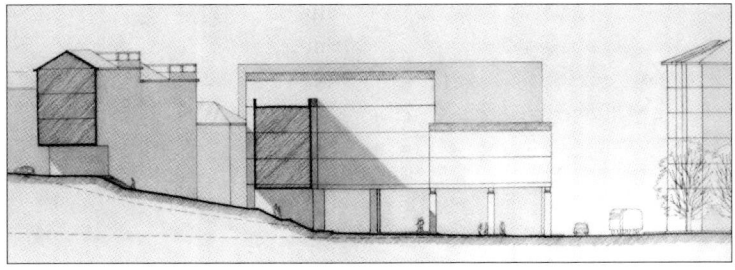

ways remain deserted. The arcades of the Prefecture in Turin are deserted, despite facing south; and in Via Po the bleakness of the University arcades, also facing south, discourage circulation on that side of the road too.[12]

The Town Council believed the arcades were necessary so that the continuity around the square would not be interrupted: Passanti accepted the suggestion despite being convinced of their functional inappropriateness, aware of the symbolic significance of continuation with the arcades on the other two sides of the square. He thus demonstrated that he was highly conversant

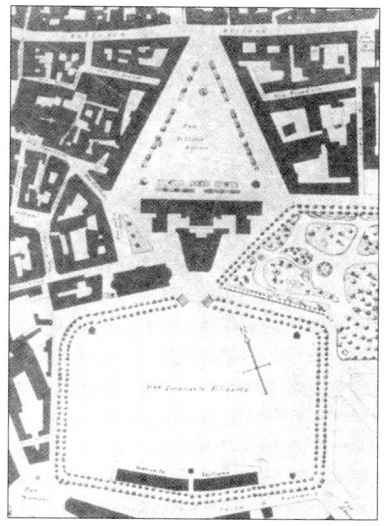

Mario Passanti and Domenico Schiavinato, Palazzo della Provincia e della Prefettura in Asti, position, 1956-1961.

with the debate about the "need for a new monumentality" that Sigfried Giedion[13] referred to, also found even more explicitly in *Nine Points on Monumentality*, by the same Giedion with Sert and Fernand Léger, from 1944 on. The seventh point specified that "people want the buildings that represent their social and community life to give more than functional fulfilment".[14] The revival of monumentality in contemporary terms allowed a wider and more accessible significance of it, which was less bound to abstract or only figurative elements and could refer to the dimension of a public space. This is significantly illustrated by the intense design focus in these years, on a European level, on the theme of civic-centres: places for studying a modern "monumentality", which was both symbolic and functional.

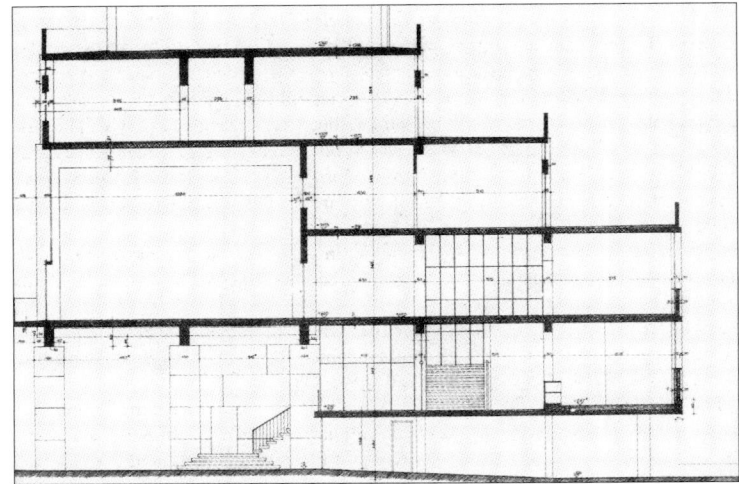

Mario Passanti and Domenico Schiavinato, Palazzo della Provincia
e della Prefettura in Asti, cross-section, 1956-1961.

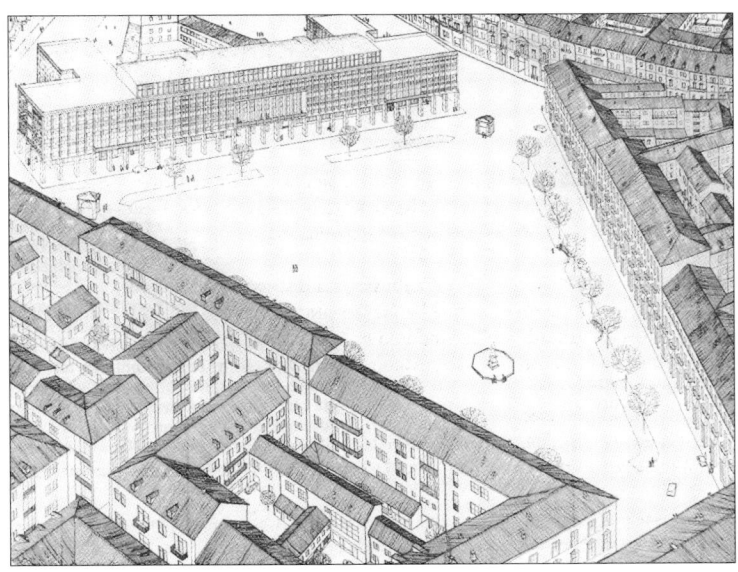

Mario Passanti and Domenico Schiavinato, Palazzo della Provincia
e della Prefettura in Asti, bird's eye view perspective, 1956-1961.

[1] M. PASSANTI, *Architettura in Piemonte: da Emanuele Filiberto all'Unità d'Italia (1563-1870)*, Libreria Tecnica Editrice, Turin 1945; republished, edited by G. TORRETTA, Allemandi, Turin 1990. Passanti's subsequent thirty-year research for *Genesi e comprensione dell'opera architettonica* led to two articles in 1954 (republished at the end of *Architettura in Piemonte* of 1990) and 1966, but the book the author was working on and which he proposed to the publisher Einaudi, was never published. See Archivio Mario Passanti [AMP], cart. A3. See also M. BONINO, *Mario Passanti Architetto: un'idea di mestiere, 1949-1964*, doctoral thesis in History of Architecture and Urbanism, Polytechnic of Turin, 2004, chap. IV.

[2] C. OLMO, "Una generazione di individui", in *Atti e rassegna tecnica della Società degli Ingegneri e degli Architetti in Torino*, monographic edition on Gino Levi-Montalcini, no. 2, LXII, December 2003, pp. 9-11.

[3] AMP, cart. C21, see drawing of 28 June 1949 with the layout of the plan of the area in which the position of the new town hall was proposed. For the Town Plan of Moncalieri see F. IRACE, *Carlo Mollino*, Electa, Milan 1989.

[4] The "Schema di Piano Regolatore della Città" of 1931 matured into the "Piano Generale di Massima Regolatore Edilizio e di Ampliamento della città di Asti", drawn up by architect Fagnoni and engineer Bianchini of Florence, delivered to the Municipal Administration in October 1934 and approved by the Podestà in April 1935.

[5] A. MELIS, "Concorso per la Casa Littoria di Asti", in *L'Architettura Italiana*, April 1934, pp. 111-124.

[6] A. M. ZORGNO, "A partire dalla città", in R. RIGAMONTI (ed.), *Mario Passanti, architetto docente universitario*, Celid, Turin 1995, pp. 184-186.

[7] Notes cited by Agostino Magnaghi during the "Seminario di Studi su Mario Passanti", see *Mario Passanti, architetto docente universitario* cit., p. 190; see the relative lecture notes in AMP, cart. A40a.

[8] *Mario Passanti, architetto docente universitario* cit., pp. 25-31.

[9] AMP, cart. C21.

[10] See *CIAM VIII, The Heart of the City. Towards the Humanization of Urban Life*, edited by J. TYRWHITT, J. L. SERT and E. N. ROGERS, Lund Humphries, London 1952. See also E. MUMFORD, *The CIAM Discourse on Urbanism 1928-1960*, Mit Press, Cambridge (Mass.) 2000.

[11] See I. DE SOLÀ-MORALES, "Le Corbusier. La dispersione dello spazio pubblico", in ID., *Decifrare l'architettura*, edited by M. BONINO, Allemandi, Turin 2001, p. 65. These themes had already been introduced by Solà-Morales in the entry "Espace public", in *Le Corbusier: une encyclopédie*, exhibition catalogue, Centre Georges Pompidou, Paris 1987.

[12] AMP, cart. A45, project report.

[13] See the essay by S. GIEDION, "The Need for a New Monumentality", in P. ZUCKER, *New Architecture and City Planning, a Symposium*, Philosophical Library, New York 1944.

[14] The 'nine points' are quoted and commented in the anthology proposed by J. OCKMAN, *Architecture Culture 1943-1968. A Documentary Anthology*, Rizzoli, New York 1993, pp. 27-30.

IV. Conceiving and building the Palazzo dei Lavori Pubblici (1956-1966)

On 23 January 1956 the Town Council approved the competition brief for the technical and administrative office building of the city's Public Works department.[1] As seen above, the chosen area in front of the Cathedral of San Giovanni had been bought the preceding year from the Municipality.

The competition brief was drafted on the basis of the Reconstruction Plan approved in July 1954.[2] Numerous architectural and functional details indicate that the Municipal Technical Office already had well defined objectives, which limited possible approaches to the project. A detailed description of all the necessary functions was included, with relative surface measurements: these seem to indicate a centrally planned building, which would be followed by the majority of participants.

Only five projects were handed in on the established date of 29 October, and all were by local groups. This was very different from the competition held by the Province in 1935 for the same area, which was entered by more than twenty groups from all over Italy. On 27 January 1957 the jury, comprising the mayor Peyron, the councillor for Public Works Anselmetti, the head of Roman Antiquities Carlo Carducci, the head of Monuments in Piedmont Umberto Chierici and representatives from the professional associations,[3] issued its verdict.

Two approaches prevailed among the projects presented: the first, represented by the groups of Giorgio and Annibale Rigotti and of Gabriele Navale, worked around a traditional closed block scheme. The other three projects (Passanti, Garbaccio and Perona; Ernesto Balistreri and Orsola De Paoli; Mario Federico Roggero with Maria Grazia Daprà Conti) were all characterised by an analogous open block 'H' plan: the

Reconstruction Plan had allowed for this type, which enabled greater building density thanks to the hygiene laws in act.[4]

In this arrangement the commission saw a reference to "essentially functional criteria" in the three projects that planned vertical links and services in a central block that united two longer parallel bodies. These criteria had been favoured by the Technical Office when drawing up a feasibility study, before the competition was proclaimed and under the responsibility of the engineer Mario Daprà, who would then be director of works of the building. Maria Grazia Conti, his future wife, debated her university thesis in 1956 with Carlo Mollino (to whom Roggero was assistant), presenting a project that took this study and the preliminary surveys carried out by the municipal offices as its starting point.[5] The 'H' scheme, the most practicable solution for including the wealth of functional elements requested, was thus present from this degree thesis, and later taken up and developed by Roggero so that it could be presented in the competition.

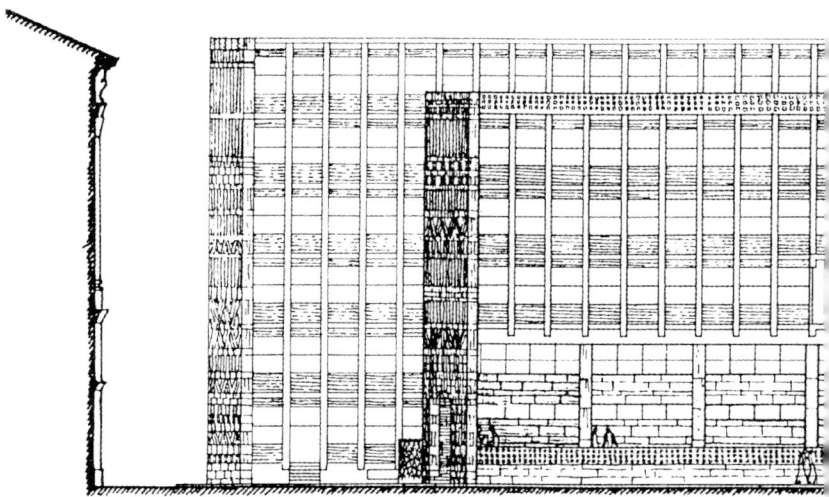

Mario Passanti, Paolo Perona and Giovanni Garbaccio, competition project for the Palazzo dei Lavori Pubblici, elevation on Piazza San Giovanni, 1956.

While acknowledging the "topical nature" of the proposals, the Commission maintained that the "difficult problem of inserting the new building into the archaeological-monumental zone had not been satisfactorily resolved by any of the participants". Regarding the proportions indicated by the Reconstruction Plan for the facade on Piazza San Giovanni, where an arcade two storeys high against only three above had been planned, "the projects [...] resort to devices for varying the relationships between the arcade and the solid volumes, lowering the solid volume itself in various ways or raising the floor of the arcade". Roggero remembers that this was the central theme for the participants: in his project the upper storeys were sustained structurally and figuratively by a large bridge frame with Vierendel beams, in which inspiration from designer engineers like Maillard (who would increasingly influence his work), under the impetus of Mollino, can be noted.[6]

No first prize was in fact awarded: second went to the project by Passanti, Perona and Garbaccio, and equal third to Roggero and to Navale.

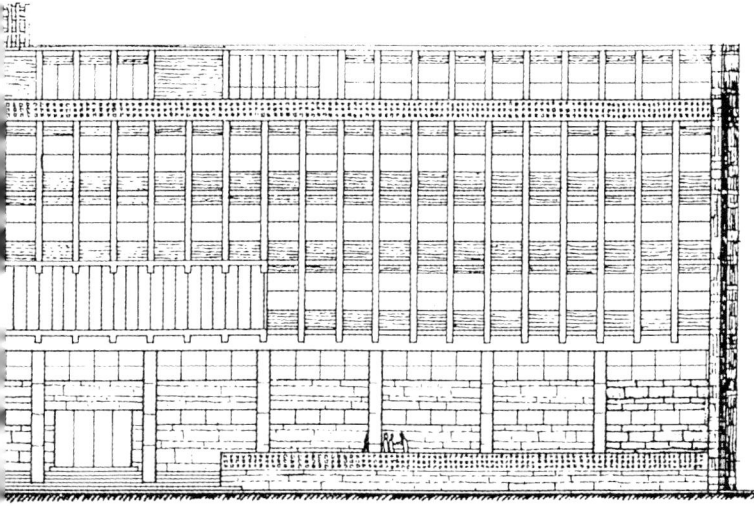

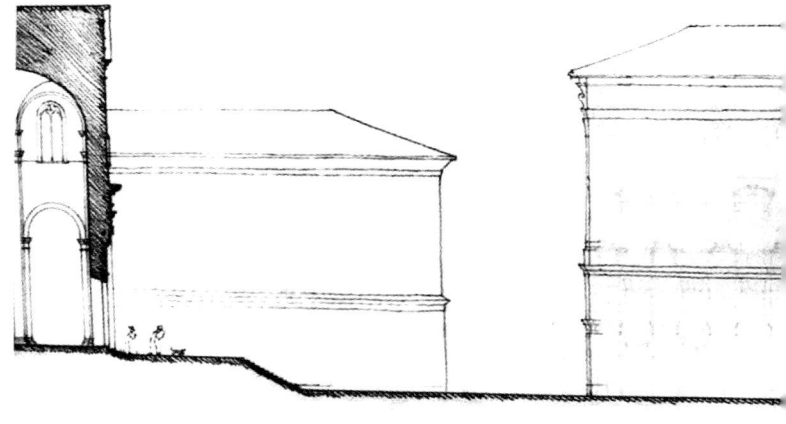

Mario Passanti, Paolo Perona and Giovanni Garbaccio,
cross-section through the building.

The latter choice was justified by the desire to bring a closed block project to the attention of the Municipality.

The project description of Passanti's group explained that the 'H' plan
layout interpreted a place where the short sides of the building looked
onto small spaces (sixteen metres Via IV Marzo, twelve metres Via della Basilica), while the two long sides looked onto large spaces, one with
a lot of traffic (behind, where the twenty-four metre-wide road crossing
the historic centre would have passed), the other with no traffic but of
huge representational importance. In this way the building allowed
"more room towards the smaller spaces", without the risk of losing, at
the same time, the important alignment of Via IV Marzo towards the
Cathedral. Regarding the difficult issue of the arcade, the report pointed out that:

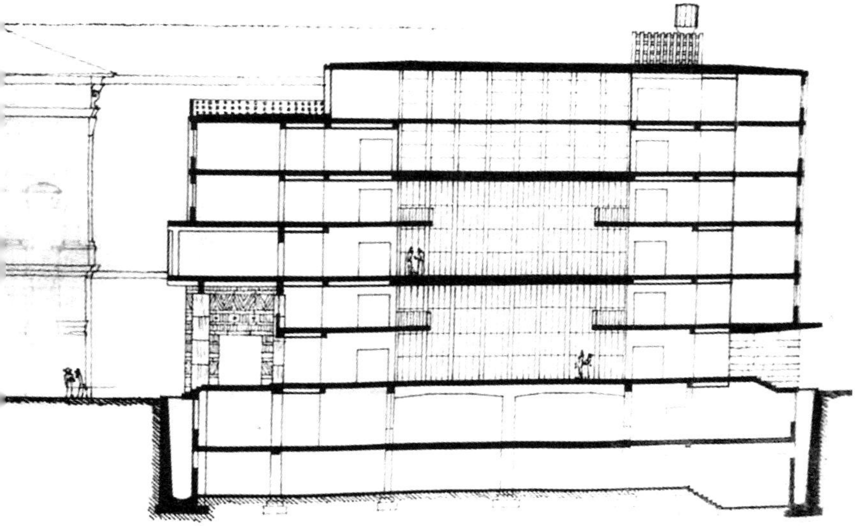

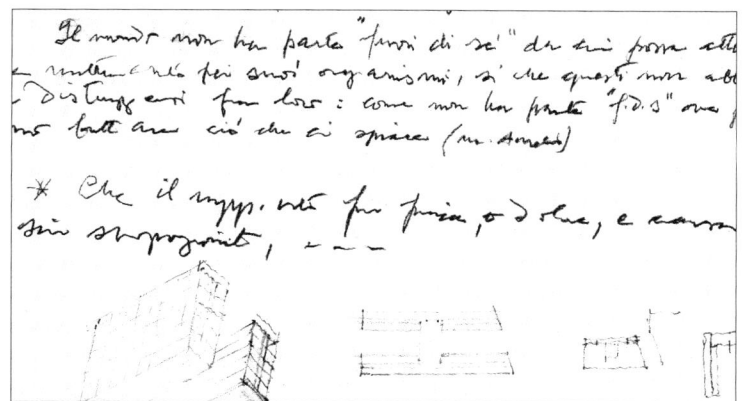

Sketch by Mario Passanti, at the bottom of lecture notes, undated. This is the 'matrix' of the project for the Palazzo dei Lavori Pubblici: this version shows the building with four straight ends, whereas the competition project proposed bevelled hexagonal ends.

The arcade of the building acting as a backdrop to functions and ceremonies held in the Cathedral square. All the early versions of the project planned for small side entrances to the arcade in order to discourage longitudinal transit.

Unlike other arcaded squares in Turin (San Carlo, Carlo Felice) the arcade towards the Cathedral square will not be traversed along its length, so consequently the end openings are not important; all the focus, instead, is directed towards the square.

In a later typewritten document, dated 13 February 1957, Mario Passanti took up a number of considerations: he described the "site and limitations", interpreting them in relation to the height of the new building, "so that linking up with the Seminario of equal height and with Palazzo Chiablese a little lower, they all create a backdrop to the Cathedral and make it stand out". He then explained:

The building's external appearance reflected the different purposes of the parts of the whole and its structure. So, every part ⁄ arcade, two⁄storey atriums, the ends of the corridors in the long wings, office areas and meeting room ⁄ appears clearly on the exterior".[7]

Different functions capable of remedying the uniform continuity of the facade design were not planned to appear on the rear facade.[8]

Years later it is still possible to deduce from a third undated report, but probably dating to the early years of the 1960s (when the building was under construction), that:

> The system of a load-bearing structure made up of uprights and superimposed floor slabs, independent from vertical closures, was chosen for its rapid execution [...] instead of the other type of load-bearing structure in iron and light-weight infill panels on a metal frame. Not only because the first cost less, but above all because its undressed surfaces of concrete and brick seemed to us to suit the site better.[9]

On 29 April 1957 the Municipal Council approved the results of the competition:[10] though they had not been proclaimed winners nor assigned the project design, Passanti, Perona and Garbaccio were once more at work by the end of May.[11] On 28 October of the same year, the Municipal Council decreed to charge the three men with the work: "In the light of particular circumstances it is believed opportune to entrust the architects of the best project with the job [...], since the site demands that particular attention is given to the architectural part in view of the environmental characteristics of Turin's archaeological area". The project would be developed "in every building and technical detail" and the Municipality reserved the right to introduce new elements, even changes. For the executive phase, the designers were charged with "architectural and artistic supervision during the execution of the work for the sake of perfect correspondence with and exact interpretation of the drawings".[12]

On 24 March 1958 the designers handed over to the Technical Office the definitive project, which included several important variations compared to the competition project:[13] the proportions between the double-height arcade and the three storeys above has remained the same, as has the division of the facade into thirty modules divided by concrete uprights, which interrupt ribbon windows and mark the points where, inside, the free-standing walls defining the work areas can be freely attached. The arched beam of the arcade makes its first appearance, one of the elements that will undergo the most changes in future versions. From a planning point of view, only the two lateral ends towards Via IV Marzo maintain their bevelled hexagonal shape, while the other two ends are

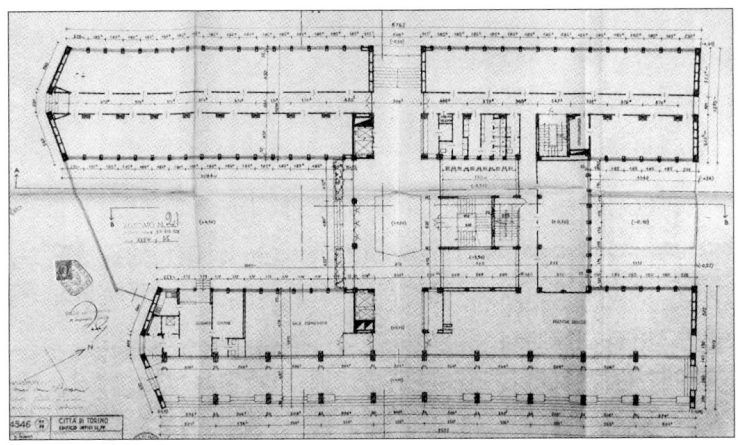

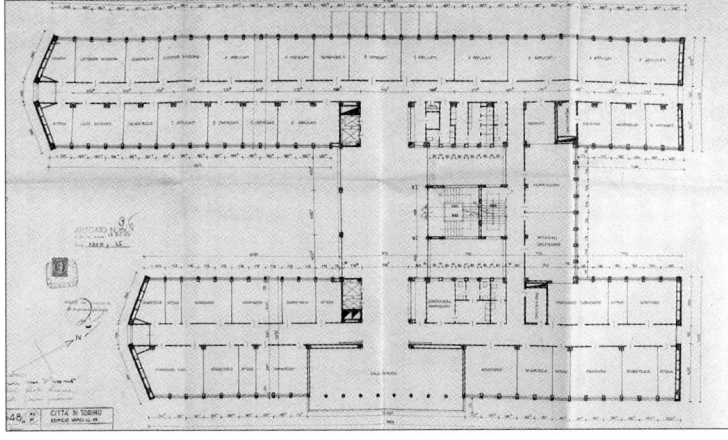

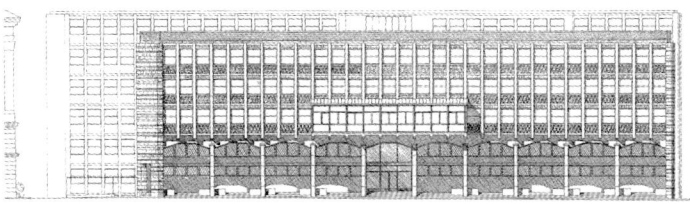

Mario Passanti, Paolo Perona and Giovanni Garbaccio, definitive project, 24 March 1958; plan of the ground floor, plan of the second floor and elevation on Piazza San Giovanni. The projecting council room stands out clearly, as in the competition project.

Photomontages of the model made in 1958, required by the municipal executive council for a better understanding of the project.

now straight: the new layout can interpret on the one side the diagonal of Via IV Marzo, centred on the Cathedral, and on the other the narrow Via della Basilica, with the facade of the Antiquities Museum planned a few metres away.

Approval from the Monuments Office on 17 May meant the work could proceed,[14] and in June the Municipal Council approved the definitive project and decreed financing for its execution.[15]

The project was the object of much discussion in the High Council of Public Works from summer 1958 through to spring of the next year: seven variations to the definitive document approved by the Town Council, all to do with the facade facing the Cathedral, were necessary to resolve this phase. A short distance from Piazza San Giovanni and in the same period, Passanti and Perona were working on the reconstruction of the building at Piazza Castello 139, destroyed by the war. For this facade on the square the architects proposed a philological reconstruction, contrasting with a contemporary rear-facing facade, not visible to the public. Contrary to Piazza San Giovanni, this approach

Mario Passanti and Paolo Perona, reconstruction of the building at Piazza Castello 139, 1952-1960; facade on the square and facade on the courtyard.

gained the immediate approval of the Superintendencies and the Ministry.

On 6 October 1958 the Secretary General of Turin's Municipality was informed that the High Council had rejected the project for the Public Works building, which had to be "re-examined and re-worked, also in view of the monumental buildings in Piazza Porta Palatina, San Giovanni, etc".[16] Pier Luigi Nervi's opinion was one of those that led to this decision, as Passanti would recall at the beginning of the 1960s:

> Nervi, a member of the Commission, raised doubts about whether it was suitable to shape the beam in the modestly sized bays of only [about five] metres with a central horizontal intrados and two short lateral diagonals, as has been done [...] This particular observation stems from a general principle, which we were not fully aware of at that time, about the relationship between an ideal form and the real dimension it refers to.[17]

On this point, Garbaccio stated that those techniques of reinforced concrete were rather elementary in that work context, before the devel-

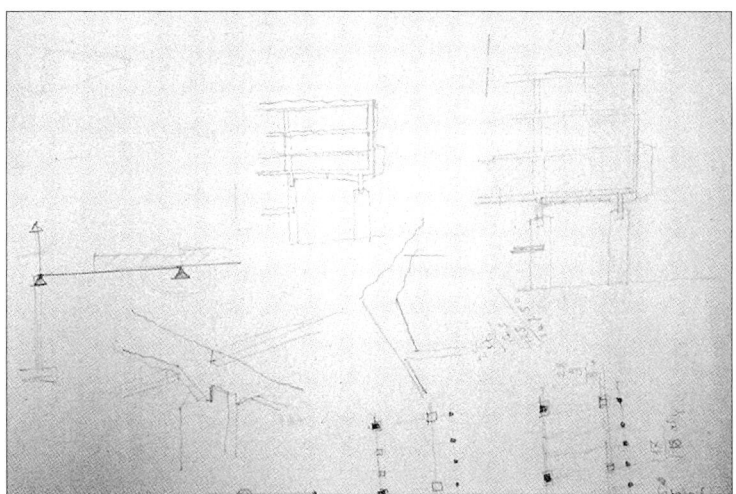

Sketches studying the building structure, undated (1958).

opments that would lead in later years to the sophisticated results to be seen in Turin's architecture.[18]

On 12 November 1958 the architects presented a first variant to the definitive project. Access to the arcade, now with a horizontal intrados as in the competition design, was via just three flights of steps located in the centre and at the ends, while the small doors at the ends disappeared completely. This proposal would be bypassed after meetings on 14 and 20 November in Rome, in the 1st Section of the High Council of Pub-

Elevation on Piazza San Giovanni, variation to the definitive project, 12 November 1958.

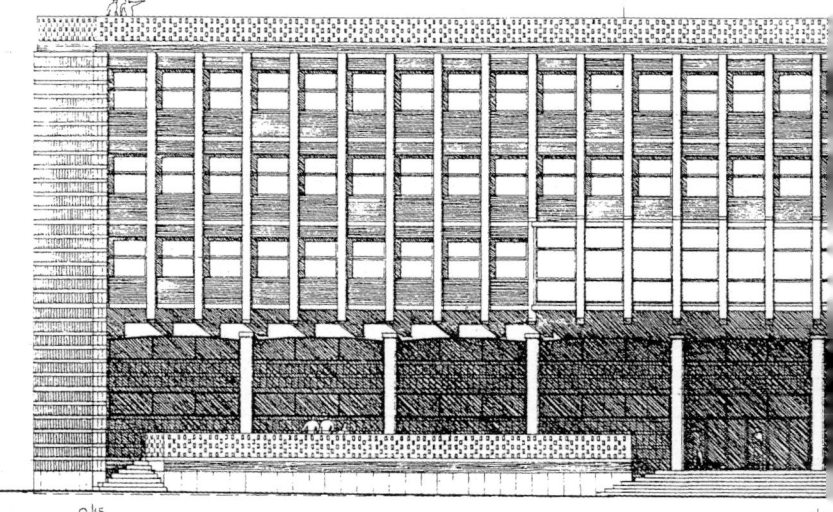

Elevation on Piazza San Giovanni, second variation to the definitive project, 2 December 1958.

lic Works: Passanti illustrated the changes made, emphasising particu-larly the "re-worked ends of the wings of the buildings, to make them less independent of the facades". With a model and an "illustrative sec-tion", it was shown that the rear wing was not visible from the parvis of San Giovanni.[19] The commissioners objected that the facade facing the Cathedral was "too perforated and too light compared to the facades of the neighbouring palaces and the church itself", believing that "a more solid facade with less surface movement would be more suitable". The Commission proposed reducing the arcade to just the central part of the building and recommended looking at a "new building in Via Quat-tro Fontane [...] between Via Nazionale and Via XX Settembre" in Rome: these were the offices of the Istituto Mobiliare Italiano - Ufficio Italiano Cambi, designed by Mario Paniconi and Giulio Pediconi of 1949-1955.

On 20 November 1958 the Commission met again (present Arnal-do Foschini and Nervi) but "the solutions proposed were not found ful-ly satisfactory".[20] The next meeting was set for 20 December. In prep-

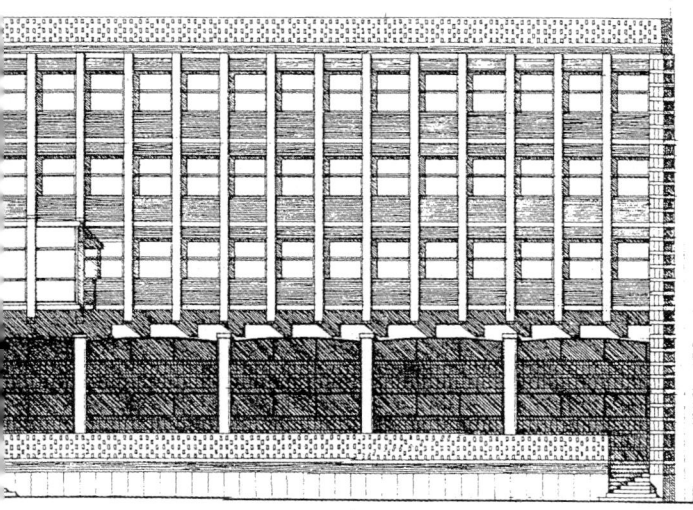

Mario Paniconi and Giulio Pediconi, with Vincenzo Passarelli, offices of the Istituto Mobiliare Italiano ⁄ Ufficio Italiano Cambi, Rome, 1949⁄1955. This building was highly recommended to Mario Passanti by the High Council of Public Works as an example for the facade on Piazza San Giovanni.

Cooperativa Architetti e Ingegneri di Reggio Emilia, office building in Rome, published by Bruno Zevi in *L'architettura. Cronache e storia*, 38, December 1958.

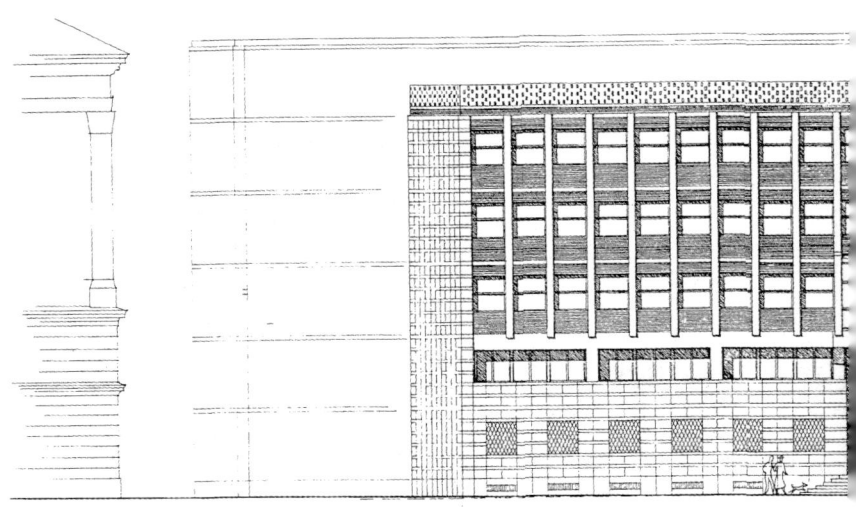

Elevation on Piazza San Giovanni, third variation to the definitive project, 12 December 1958.

aration for this meeting, two alternative variations for the facade on Piazza San Giovanni were drawn up on 2 and 9 December: in the first, the
scheme was very similar to the version of 12 November, but greater ex-
pressive powers had been given to the structural elements, with the beam
of the arcade once again shaped; in the second, instead, the arcade disappeared and the facade arrived at ground level, with the entrance to the
offices positioned in just three central bays, as in the building in Via
Quattro Fontane in Rome.

On 12 December, however, Passanti, Perona and Garbaccio drafted
a new version, where a large central opening was still reserved for the entrance. This solution, as in those of a few years earlier, recalls the first version for the Palazzo della Provincia e Prefettura in Asti, designed by Passanti in November 1955.

During the meeting of 20 December further solutions were requested:

The Council noted that the double-height arcade requested in the competition brief, combined with opportunely raising it above the level of the
square, created a height that was little less than the three storeys above; in-

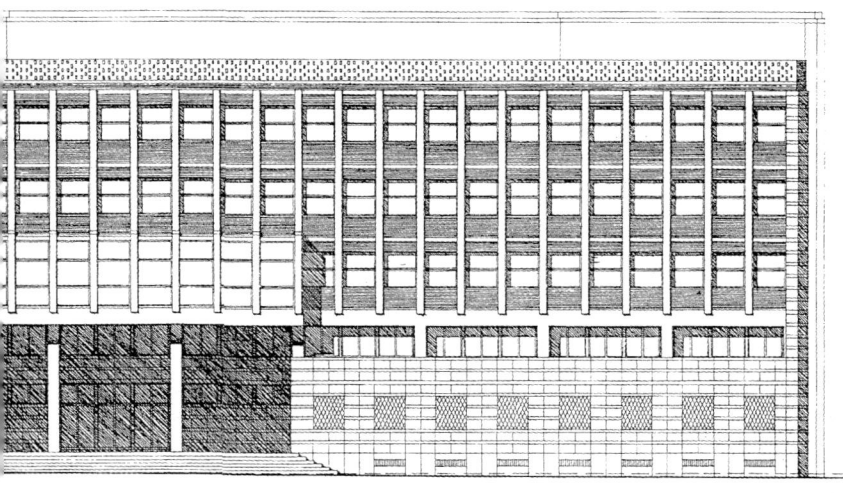

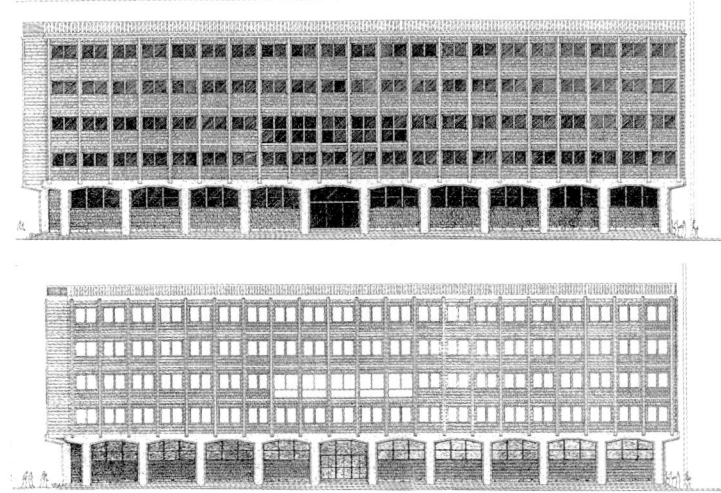

Variations of 27 February 1959 (B) and of 14 March 1959.

stead, the front would have better proportions if the arcade were reduced just to the height of the ground floor, thus emphasising the difference between its void and the solid of the four storeys above more strongly. Having changed the competition brief in this manner, we believe fittingly, the Council invited us to present further proposals.[21]

While a version of 27 February 1959 (A) still included the choices and proportions of the proposal of 12 November (the only substantial difference being the disappearance of the projecting council room), a parallel solution (B) instead presented significant new ideas. For the first time the arcade was only one storey high, and the uprights divided the facade into twenty bays, instead of the previous thirty. The beam in the end bays now projected over the arcade and this device perfected the rhythm of the staggered alignments of the uprights with respect to the axis of the arcade piers. This was borrowed directly from a Roman office building, designed by the Cooperativa Architetti e Ingegneri of Reggio Emilia, recently published by Bruno Zevi in *L'architettura. Cronache e storia* (38) two months earlier, in December 1958.

The asymmetry of the entrance and the council room compared to the overall facade was instead maintained. The connecting volume on the roof also remained asymmetrical, in an opposite sense. This sophisticated play on the composition of an asymmetrical facade, due to the axes of the entrance to the building and to the Cathedral not corresponding to the symmetrical axis of the square, was one of the newest elements compared to the project for the Asti building, and not only on a formal level: it derived from a more complex and structured way of interpreting the context. The crowning element defining the public terrace towards Piazza San Giovanni was also modified, although temporarily: the alternating brick pattern of the parapet creating a sort of *treillage* now became vertical slits, designed by Passanti to provide a more transparent view from the street.

The architects were asked for a further modification to this last version, which they presented to the High Council on 14 March 1959. The system of windows now lost its horizontal continuity, interrupted up till then only by the uprights which the internal wall divisions corresponded to, and every window was squarely framed. On 18 March, Sections I and IV of the High Council of Public Works considered the project worthy of approval, despite making some observations:[22] their resolution was deferred to the regional Office head and to the discussions he had from now on with the High Council of Antiquities and Fine Arts, standing in for the Ministry of Education. Another three versions, focusing almost exclusively on the facade towards Piazza San Giovanni would be produced during the discussions with this new interlocutor: meanwhile, the executive project was proceeding in forced stages.[23]

Following the Public Works Council's approval, the architects produced a complete new version, delivered on 30 April 1959 to the Municipal Technical Office.[24] On 3 July, the head of Monuments in Piedmont Chierici sent these plates to the Ministry of Education, expressing uncertainty about "the merits of the new facade design, since its monotony and proportions do not seem satisfactorily suitable for being inserted into the surrounding monumental context".[25]

On 20 July, Passanti, when visiting the Director General's office of Antiquities and Fine Arts in Rome which had asked for further information, made it known that "the Director General of Fine Arts, professor De Angelis d'Ossat, was a member of the High Council of Public Works and that he was one of the authors of the High Council's report".[26] The session of the High Council of Antiquities and Fine Arts, in which the subject was to be discussed, was held only on 7 October 1959; more clarification from the architects was deemed necessary before an assessment could be made.

Accompanied by Perona and Garbaccio, on 21 October Passanti went to Rome for a long talk with Vittorio Ballio Morpurgo, president and speaker of the Commission.

> Morpurgo asked to have a meeting with the designers in which views could be exchanged, as occurs among simple colleagues [...] He believes that the lengths and heights of the two long bodies should be made equal [...] At our objection that the alignment of the volumes on Via IV Marzo would be lost, which seems crucial to us, he replied that a low volume could be

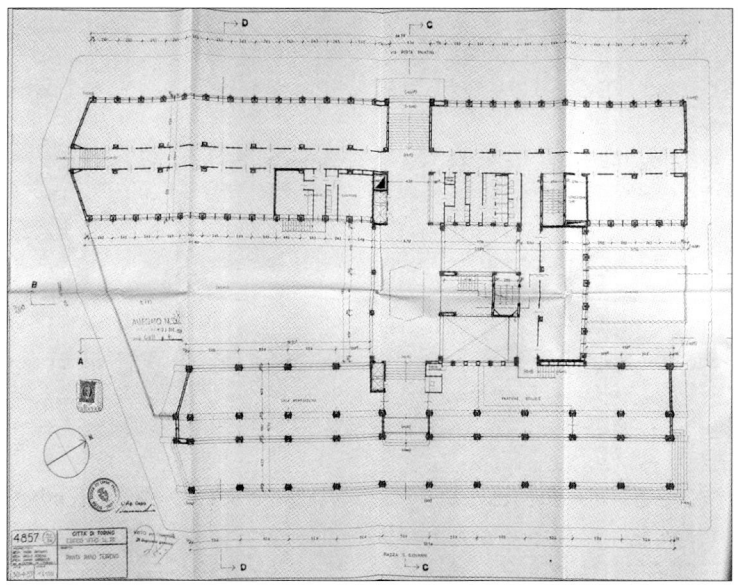

Revision of the definitive project after the Town Council vote, plan of the ground floor, 30 April 1959.

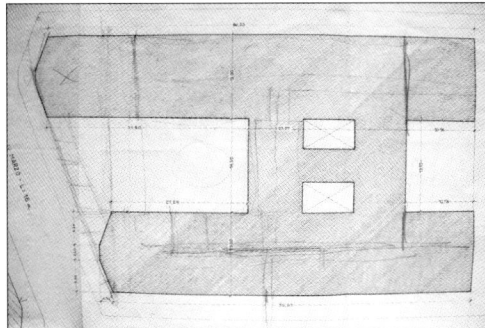

Memo drafted by
Mario Passanti after
the meeting of 21 October
1959 with Vittorio Ballio
Morpurgo.

The plan used to
support the discussion.

set along that street. At the objection that this would greatly reduce the cu‑
bic volume, he replied that perhaps it was possible to raise the central part.

Instead, in the architects' opinion, "it was more appropriate to streng‑
then the alignment, creating a tall, possibly pierced, wing along the
street".

Subsequent to their Roman visit, Passanti, Perona and Garbaccio
drew up a new version, dated 27 November, which replaced the draw‑
ings of 30 April: the rear wing was now given an attic storey, to bring
the parapet level to the same height on all sides of the building.[27]

After the meeting with Morpurgo, Garbaccio was witness to other
lengthy discussions with the High Council of Antiquities and Fine Arts,
in an attempt to eliminate the whole of the top floor of the rear wing, a pro‑
posal never put to paper though.[28] The architects themselves proposed and
were authorised, in 1961, to abandon the solution drafted in November.

The minutes of a new meeting of the High Council, of 27 November, was not signed and left open:

The question that had been dealt with by the High Council in the session of 7 October 1959 [...] The Section [...] had deferred making a decision, believing it essential to have clarification beforehand, preferably directly from the architects. The Section [...] decides that an on site examination should be made by all its members.

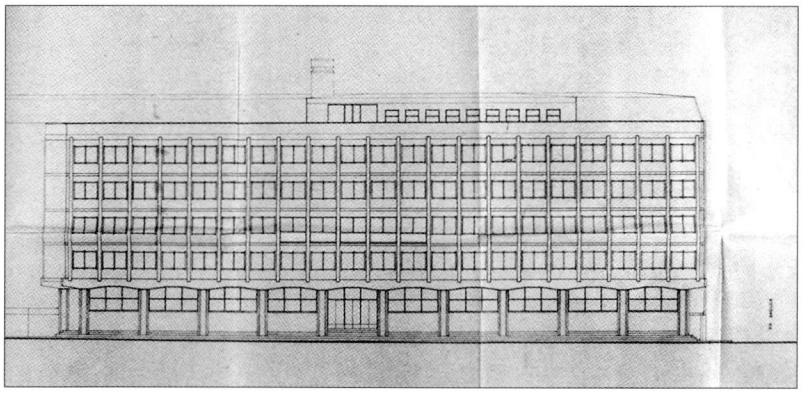

Elevation on Piazza San Giovanni, variation of 27 November 1959.
There is now an attic storey on the rear wing.

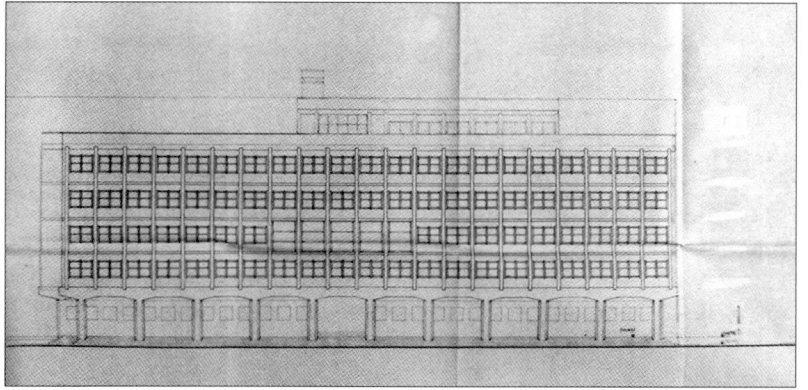

The variation of July 1961, definitively approved by the municipal executive council.

After the visit on site in Turin, the drawings were sent, on 2 December, by the Monuments Office to the Municipality. However, "a reserve is made to agree the details pertaining to materials and decorative elements with the designers and the said Municipality at the moment of execution".[29]

Passanti summarised some aspects of this last version with respect to the first ideas for the project:

> In the project that was finally approved every wing was homogeneous, with a reinforced concrete frame and brick infill. But the feeling of external continuity, or office flexibility, was lost, since the uninterrupted bands of glass had been replaced by individual windows.[30]

On 21 December 1959 the definitive approval of the Town Council was recorded.[31] The Christian Democrat majority (Giancarlo Anselmetti was still councillor for Public Works, and would be mayor from February 1962) obtained approval for procedures for private tendering for the masonry work and, despite violent criticism from the opposition led by Alberto Todros, all the work was contracted out using this mechanism.

The work began in November 1960, but was halted by decree on 28 June 1961, in order to assess important changes to the top floor. Indeed, in early February, the architects drafted a variation that replaced the definitive project and relative executive plan of 16 December. On 17 May, Anselmetti sent the new version to the Monuments Office, asking for authorisation.[32] As the minutes of the Town Council, which accepted the executive council's resolution of 14 July, explains:

> The office building in Piazza San Giovanni is at an advanced stage of construction [...] The architects have now proposed changes to the architectural design of the fifth floor of the wing towards Via Porta Palatina, for aesthetic reasons. This floor, already designed as a separate architectural element from the floor below, would now have the same characteristics.[33]

Model of the definitive solution.

The proposal was re-drafted with drawings dated 7 July 1961, and work recommenced at the beginning of August.[34] From the calculations and drawings for the reinforced concrete, coordinated by the firm itself but drafted by prestigious structural engineers,[35] the progress of the building can be judged: the static schemes for the foundations date to December 1960, while calculations for the roof date to 12 September 1961.

The work proceeded with various stops, one of which was caused by the preservation group Italia Nostra occupying the site for several days.[36]

The building in its final stages; view from the north of the ends overlooking the archaeological zone.

The final designs were produced by the studio in July 1963 and the last inspection was made in May 1966, by Cesare Bairati.[37]

The project and building site of the Palazzo dei Lavori Pubblici, in Piazza San Giovanni, dragged on for more than ten years, from the proclamation of the competition in 1956 to the final inspections. The 274 plates carefully numbered by Mario Passanti, Paolo Perona and Giovanni Garbaccio, and the numerous resolutions of the municipal executive council, the Town Council, state offices and ministries reveal the complexity of the process and the huge number of decision makers involved.

Commonly known by the rather denigratory name of "palazzaccio", over the years in public opinion the building has become a landmark for a debated architectural and political sensitivity regarding the city's monu‑mental heritage. But it raises several more profound questions: how much room for manoeuvre did the designers have in the face of seemingly pre‑destined functional models (the feasibility study drawn up the Techni‑cal Office) or formal models (the facade of the public office building in Rome "highly recommended" to Passanti)? How could the architects have effectively influenced all those inconclusive meetings and post‑ponements, or have influenced the possibilities for a design relationship with a place that was being constantly changed by political and social

The facade on Piazza San Giovanni photographed from the Cathedral in 1966.

The facade on Piazza San Giovanni before restoration in 2005.

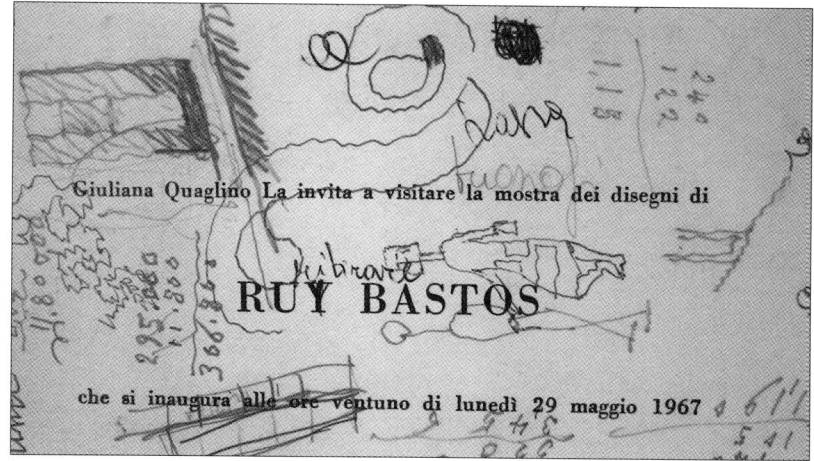

Sketch by Mario Passanti datable to 1967. In the top left, there is a 'rethinking' of the court towards Via IV Marzo.

factors? And the questions also, paradoxically, concern the much too fragmented but perhaps possible resistance of an idea of civic architecture, which obstinately seemed to re-emerge throughout the various phases of the project.

Already while the building was under construction, Passanti reflected on the results of his work: he realised that the restrictions surrounding the project in Piazza San Giovanni could be a stimulus:

> They offer opportunities and pose limits; in short they define a sphere, without which conception is impossible, and within which it is possible in a vast number of ways, - according to its author [...] Who, though, when he conceives his work in a given period, is forced to abandon those abstract possibilities and see his own idea as the only one possible.[38]

Passanti would return to reflect many times on the conception of this building, in later years, among self-criticism and polemical debate.[39] As he related during the conference on the historic city centre of 25-27 March 1966, with a controversial urban insertion the underlying choices remained, however, clearly visible. The building had simply to state on the exterior its arrangement and functions: this holds good for the geo-

Mario Passanti in the garden of his villa in San Vito, Turin, late 1950s.

metrical divisions of the facade, which aim to illustrate a horizontal rather than hierarchical view of work; for emphasising those places that allude to transparency in decision making (the glassed council room); and for the use of the same materials used in buildings in suburbs that were more than doubling in size. And all this in front of the city's traditional power nucleus, thus suggesting through contrast a new way of dialoguing with the city.

[1] Archivio Storico della Città di Torino [ASCT], Verbali Consiglio Comunale [VCC], 23 January 1956, §51, *Approvazione bando di pubblico concorso*.

[2] ASCT, VCC, 23 January 1956, §51. See all. 38, *Bando di Concorso per il progetto di massima dell'edificio per gli Uffici dei lavori pubblici del comune di Piazza San Giovanni*. Summaries of the regulations of the Reconstruction Plan relating to this area are quoted. "The block between the Cathedral square and the streets IV Marzo, Porta Palatina and Basilica will have arcaded fronts overlooking the square of the Cathedral to a height of two storeys above ground with a further three storeys above. The height will be decided by the Monuments Office and the Civic Administration to safeguard the environmental factor and to show off the Cathedral to best advantage together with the ensemble of the existing Palazzo Chiablese and the Seminario. The front towards Via Porta Palatina can be higher but in no case must exceed 21 metres".

[3] The jury also included four members nominated by the Municipality: Giovanni Bernocco, Luigi Buffa, Giacomo Dumontel and Maria Vernetti.

[4] ASCT, Miscellanea Lavori Pubblici, 726: "The new buildings can therefore be of a closed type; however, this does not exclude the Municipal Administration asking for an open or half-open type if this would be possible in the overall picture of the block".

[5] Interview with Mario Daprà, 29 March 2004, in his house, Turin.

[6] Interview with Mario Federico Roggero, 2 December 2003, in his studio, Turin.

[7] The reports relating to the competition are in Archivio Mario Passanti [AMP], cartt. C41 and A45 ("Relazioni su progetti propri"). The typewritten manuscript of 1957 is also present in cart. A45.

[8] Interview with Giovanni Garbaccio, 29 March 2004, in his studio, Turin.

[9] AMP, cart. A45, undated typewritten report.

[10] ASCT, VCC, 29 April 1957, §26, *Concorso per il progetto di massima. Esito, premi e compensi. Approvazione*.

[11] Archivio Giovanni Garbaccio [AGG], *Registro disegni dello studio*, volume 3 (from 26 February 1953 to 1 July 1961).

[12] ASCT, VCC, 28 October 1957, §13. See all. 32, *Affidamento a Passanti, Perona, Garbaccio dell'incarico della progettazione e della consulenza architettonica. Convenzione. Approvazione*.

[13] AMP, cart. C41, drawings 4546 and ff.; ASCT, VCC, 16 June 1958, §45, all. 21 and ff.

[14] Archivio della Divisione Gestione e Manutenzione del Patrimonio del Comune di Torino [ADGMPCT], 17 May 1958, no. 1427, *Lettera di approvazione della Sovrintendenza dei Monumenti del Piemonte*.

[15] ASTC, VCC, 16 June 1958, §45, *Consiglio. Approvazione del progetto. Finanziamento*. See all. 16-42. According to calculations the total budget planned amounted to 518,562.459 lire of which 88,434.000 were for the structures in reinforced concrete. The undressed concrete fronts were to be vibrated and hammered.

[16] ADGMPCT, cart. 14592.

[17] AMP, cart. A45, undated typewritten report.

[18] Interview with Giovanni Garbaccio, 29 March 2004.

[19] ADP, cart. 14592, *Promemoria circa la riunione avvenuta in Roma il 14 novembre 1958*, drafted by Passanti.

[20] ADGMPCT, cart. 14592, *Promemoria circa la riunione avvenuta in Roma il 20 novembre 1958*,

drafted by Passanti.

[21] AMP, cart. A45, undated typewritten report.

[22] Archivio del Consiglio Superiore dei Lavori Pubblici [ACSLP], *Voto del Consiglio Superiore dei Lavori Pubblici*, ession of 18.3.1959, ref. no. 1740/524. On the version approved by the Commission of 14 March, these observations were noted: "1) The architectural unity conferred on the main facade must also be ensured for the other parts of the building, consequently it would be advisable to continue the unifying architectural bands of the basement and roofing [...]; 2) the relief effects of the pilasters of the main front must be lessened to avoid them creating the idea that they are artificial elements superimposed on the facade structures". The sum approved came to 550 million lire, compared to the 300 initially estimated by the Municipal Council proclaiming the competition. See also ASCT, VCC, 21 December 1959, §96. Reference is quoted of the High Council of Public Works' approval.

[23] The drawings by Passanti, Perona and Garbaccio discussed in this chapter can be found in AMP, cart. C41. It is possible to construct their precise chronology by consulting volumes 3 and 4 of the studio's drawing records book, in AGG.

[24] AMP, cart. C41, drawings 4855/4870; see also ASCT, VCC, 21 December 1958, §96, all. 40 and ff.

[25] Archivio Centrale dello Stato, Fondo Ministero Pubblica Istruzione, Direzione Generale per le Antichità e le Belle Arti [ACS], Ufficio conservazione monumenti 1952/1959, B323, Rome.

[26] ADP, cart. 14592, memorandum drafted by Passanti on 17 September 1959.

[27] AMP, cart. C41, drawings 5071/5075; see also ASCT, VCC, 21 December 1958, §96, all. 46 and ff.

[28] Interview with Giovanni Garbaccio, 30 April 2003, Turin.

[29] ACS, MPI, AA.BB.AA., Ufficio conservazione monumenti, B323, 16 January 1960.

[30] AMP, cart. A45, undated typewritten report.

[31] ASCT, VCC, 21 December 59, §96. Later, on 20 June 1960, the council approved the estimated metric calculations updated from the executive e project.

[32] Ibid.

[33] ASCT, VCC, 17 July 1961, §97, *Approvazione variante al VI piano fuori terra della manica porte palatine*.

[34] The minutes of 1 August 1961 authorise the work to recommence.

[35] ACP, cart. 18592. Guido Benzi and Cesare Castiglia (Polytechnic of Turin) were responsible.

[36] Interview with Marcello Vindigni, 15 October 2003.

[37] ADP, cart. 6727.

[38] AMP, cart. A45, project report, p. 2.

[39] Some notes, for example, state: "greater difficulty in conception, in view of the undefined site: behind, a large road; in front, a shapeless square facing north (see instead Asti)". AMP, cart. A, pencil notes on the back of a typewritten text, relative to the project of the Public Works building, undated, probably from the early 1960s. In the final version of his never published *Genesi e comprensione dell'opera architettonica*, Passanti proposed the building as a case study and maintained that "for whoever goes from Via IV Marzo towards the square, this creates a great void on the left that distracts attention from

the space of the square and from the marvellous view of the two domes high above the mass of the Cathedral. It can also be seen on the interior how the parapets in brickwork, instead of railings in iron or glass, block the perspective of the corridors". See also the sketched plan dating to 1967 that shows the closure of the court along Via IV Marzo, see AMP, cart. A.

© 2006 UMBERTO ALLEMANDI & C., TURIN

DESKTOP PUBLISHING ROSARIO PAVIA

FOTOLITO FOTOMEC, TURIN

PRINTED IN THE MONTH OF FEBRUARY 2006

BY STAMPATRE, TURIN